The Student Leader Guidebook:

HOW TO ESTABLISH, STRENGTHEN AND MAINTAIN
A STUDENT ORGANIZATION

© ESANi
Copyright 2009
ESANi.Books@gmail.com

COVER DESIGNER: Anna Kristine Roth

Copyright 2009 © ESANi. All rights Reserved

No part of this publication may be produced, stored in a retrieval system or transmitted in any form or by any means, electronic, mechanical, photocopying, recording, scanning or otherwise, except as permitted under Sections 107 or 108 of the 1976 United States Copyright Act, without either the prior written permission of ESANi, or authorization through payment of the appropriate per-copy fee to the Copyright Clearance Center, Inc. 222 Rosewood Drive, Danvers, MA 01923, (508) 750-4470. Requests to ESANi for permission should be addressed by email to ESANi.Books@gmail.com.

To order books or enquire about the content, please email at: ESANi.Books@gmail.com

ISBN - 978-0-578-01529-3

Special Thanks To...

those who made this book possible – We could not have done this without your support

Anna Kristine Roth
for cover design

Hilda Coleman
for initial editing

Kathleen Paonessa Roth
for final editing

Aaron Haight & Michelle Burke
for concept generation/ organization

Daniel Royer
for publishing/ printing guidance

Grand Valley State University
for providing us with the experiences and opportunities necessary to write this book

Table of Contents

FOREWORD	I
INTRODUCTION	II
SECTION 1 – ESTABLISHING YOUR ORGANIZATION: MISSION, GOALS, PROGRAMS AND MEMBERSHIP	1
DEFINE YOUR ORGANIZATION	2
Am I the right leader for this organization?	3
Do I have a clear understanding of what constitutes my organization?	4
ESTABLISH AN ORGANIZATIONAL STRUCTURE	8
Leadership Structure – "The Core 4"	9
Membership Involvement	12
SET YOUR GOALS ACCORDING TO YOUR MISSION	14
Long Term vs. Short Term Goals	15
Associate a Time Frame for Your Goals	15
Sculpt Organizational Programs Around These Goals	16
Defining Failure and Continuous Improvement	17
RECRUIT MEMBERS	20
Numbers and Personality	21
"Meet and Greet"	21
Attract Members	22
Uncomfortable Recruiting	23
SECTION 2 – STRENGTHENING YOUR ORGANIZATION: BUILDING UNITY, MAINTAINING ORDER, RETAINING MEMBERSHIP AND PROMOTING A POSITIVE IMAGE	25
BUILD UNITY	26
Teambuilding	27
Unity	29
Sharing	30
Support	31

CONDUCT A PROPER MEETING	**32**
Before Any Meeting	33
Core 4 Meetings	34
General Body Meetings	37
ESTABLISH A PURPOSE FOR MEMBERSHIP	**42**
New Members	43
Meeting Substance	43
Member Roles and Responsibilities	44
Keep it Positive	45
Flexibility	45
SPREAD THE WORD: POSITIVE PROMOTION AND ADVERTISING	**48**
Importance of Promotion and Advertising	49
Ways of Promoting and Advertising: Pt.1	49
Ways of Promoting and Advertising: Pt.2	51
Ethics and Advertising	52
Conclusion	54
SECTION 3 - MAINTAINING YOUR ORGANIZATION: BUDGETING, FUNDRAISING, NETWORKING, AND DEVELOPING NEW OFFICERS	**55**
BUDGET YOUR MONEY	**56**
Requesting Money	57
Money Allocation	58
Budget Tweaking	59
Key Player	60
FUNDRAISE FOR ACTIVITIES	**62**
Why Do You Need Fundraisers?	63
Planning	63
Fundraiser Sizes and Types	64
Additional Considerations	66
Advertising	68
Paperwork	68
SET UP A NETWORK	**70**
Faculty and Staff Respect/Assistance	71
Peer Respect and Networking	72
National Respect	74

PASS THE TORCH	**76**
Choosing New Officers	77
Forcing Members to Become Leaders	79
Preparation	80
Staying Active After Leadership	81
TROUBLESHOOTING – PROBLEM IDENTIFICATION	**84**
The 5 Whys	84
Finding the Optimal Solution	87
Appendix 1: Fundraising List	**89**
Appendix 2: Budget Example	**90**
Appendix 3: Agenda Example	**92**
Appendix 4: Program Checklist Example	**95**
Appendix 5: Flier Example	**98**

Foreword

During the final weeks of our undergraduate careers, the authors of this book sat down to discuss what the next steps in our lives were to be. It is difficult to be so active in your campus community and then leave it all behind after graduation. We found success in our collegiate careers: we obtained good grades, received several awards, and graduated with the respect of our peers and school administration. We ran a student organization that we rebuilt. When we took over leadership responsibilities, the organization's presence on campus was dismal. When we finished, it was one of the most respected organizations on campus.

As we graduated, we asked ourselves how could we pass on to the new leaders of our organization the knowledge which we had gained? We expanded this idea to include all campus organizations. We were certain that others could benefit from the knowledge and experience that we obtained over our collegiate careers. So, we developed an idea of writing a book about starting and operating a successful student organization. We spoke with staff at our Office of Student Life and asked about the material that existed for training student leaders. We did not want to reinvent the wheel if there was something already out there. We were given some books to read but were told that none of them were all inclusive. Our goal was to write one manual that contained all the information to create and sustain any campus organization. We decided to write something that clearly detailed the things that a new or established student leader needs to know in order to start or continue leading a student organization.

Introduction

The audience for this book is student leaders who need help starting or continuing to lead a student organization. From what we have seen, students do not begin college with knowledge and experience in running student organizations unless they have had extensive experience in high school. Unfortunately, in most instances, there is not one concrete resource that says, "Do this, this, and this to make your organization successful." Typically someone has to go through some experiences first before he/she truly knows how to be a leader. So the question we asked ourselves was "What if, from the start, a student leader knew what to do?" "How much more successful would student organizations be if the inexperienced leaders knew from the beginning how to be successful." This is the goal that we have worked towards in writing this book. We hope you find the book insightful and helpful on your leadership journey.

This book is intend to be a guide for those inexperienced leaders. There are no exact answers to questions of how to organize and run your specific organization. Experience will always be the best learning tool. However, what we have provided are method, suggestions, and questions that you as the leader of your student organization should consider. We also intended this book to be used for many types of organizations. If you look at an athletic club and an environmental group, the only difference between them is the mission of the organization and the specific programs. Both organizations need members, money to fund programs, and a reason to exist on campus. So, a leader of either organization is able to find valuable information in this book and we hope you find it valuable as well. If you follow the simple three phase process presented in this book – Establish, Strengthen, and Maintain – you and your organization are destined for success.

Section 1 – Establishing your Organization:

Mission, Goals, Programs, and Membership

DEFINE YOUR ORGANIZATION

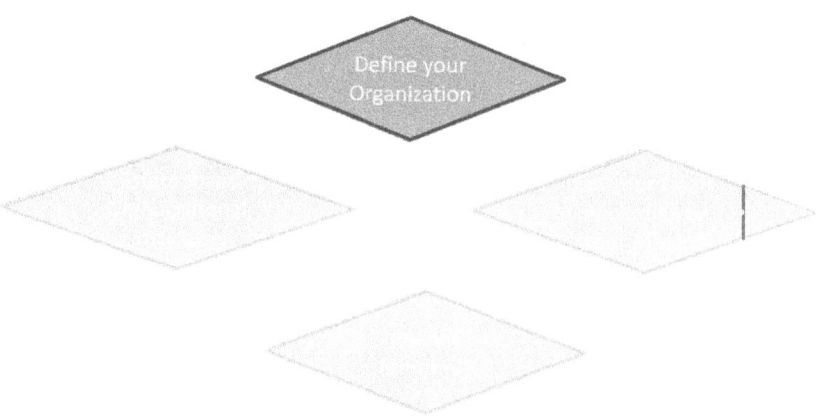

        Student organizations provide a different aspect of college life that the classroom cannot offer. Students who take part in organizations are proven to be more rounded individuals when entering the work world. In college, it is important for students to join different types of organizations to maximize their college experience. Finding an organization of which you have a passion is a good choice. Furthermore, you should consider if the organization will be a fun and rewarding experience for you. In some cases, it is not necessary for you to understand the ins and outs of an organization, or know if it is a good fit before joining. However, if you are planning to lead or start an organization you need to have a different mindset.

DEFINE YOUR ORGANIZATION

In order to lead an organization you need to answer two questions:

(1) Am I the right leader for this organization?
(2) Do I have a clear understanding of this organization?

The following is the thinking process that you should know before venturing out on your first leadership journey. This process is the same whether you are just starting an organization, or becoming a leader of one that you have been a member of for some time.

Am I the right leader for this organization?

You cannot be a leader of an organization if you do not feel comfortable in the role. A leader's purpose is to guide his or her members to success; and if you are unsure of yourself, it will be difficult to do this. An effective leader must always have a clear understanding of direction and goals. The steps for actually setting goals are discussed in Step 3: Set Your Goals and Plan Accordingly. The leader must ask himself or herself some basic questions before setting goals, such as *Is the organization something to which I can relate? Do I have a passion for it?*

For example, if you hate math, you probably should not be the captain of the algebra team. If you have no passion for politics, the president of student government is not the job for you. These are obvious examples of an organization that is not right for you. Please understand that in order to join an organization only an interest is required, but to lead an organization you must have strong convictions and a solid passion.

A leader must be passionate about his or her organization's purpose and want to lead others to fulfill that purpose. You cannot expect people to follow a passionless leader. Passion shows confidence to your members and gives them the belief that this is not only something you want to do, but something they should do as well. Make sure that you have a strong connection to the group, a passion to lead, and a clear vision of its purpose and mission. If you have these skills, you are a perfect fit for this organization's leadership position.

Do I have a clear understanding of what constitutes my organization?

The most important step in starting or running an organization is defining what your group will actually be doing. What is your group's purpose? Why do people want to join your organization? If the purpose and membership benefits are not firmly established before your journey, then your organization will fail. So, to begin defining your organization, here are three major questions that all leaders must answer before starting or leading an organization. What is the purpose of this organization? Is there a need for this organization on campus? Who is the organization going to benefit, and how?

Defining purpose – Mission Statement

Every leader needs to be able to define his/her organization in a brief and concise way. The easiest way to do this is to create a mission statement. A mission statement is an easy-to-remember sentence, short list of bullet points, or paragraph illustrating a group's purpose. It sets the tone for your organization and has one function: to guide you and your members in making critical decisions that affect the direction of your organization. If your organization already has a mission statement, make

DEFINE YOUR ORGANIZATION

sure that it does this and that you fully understand it. Disney's mission statement is an excellent example: *"To make people happy[1]"*

It is simple, but would anybody argue that Disney accomplishes this? No. Do you think it sets the tone? Yes. The employees at Disney follow their mission to create a happy experience for their customers. When starting a new organization, understand what it is you want your group to accomplish. Decide on a description that is simple, promotes a positive image, and will guide the behavior of your membership. If your organization already has a mission statement that does this, then be sure to always operate with it in mind and always readdress it when necessary.

Determining a Need on Campus

Once you have your purpose defined, your next step is determining the need for your organization on campus. The easiest way to determine this is to research the other organizations that already exist on campus. Make sure that other groups on campus do not have the same purpose as yours. Contact your student organization center to obtain a list of the student groups in your category (Academic, Athletic, Greek, etc). Then check to see if another organization on campus is not already fulfilling the need you are trying to satisfy. In your search one of three scenarios will present themselves. (1) There is no other organization on campus like yours; (2) there is one or a few that are similar but slightly different; or (3) there is a group exactly like yours. If there are no groups like yours, then you have defined your need on campus and should continue with your efforts. If there is a group or a few groups that are similar, then you should probably redefine your purpose to ensure you are not duplicating efforts. If there is a group that is identical, you should rethink the need for your

---

[1]Disney, www.corporate.disney.go.com (2008)

SECTION 1:
ESTABLISH YOUR ORGANIZATION

organization and possibly join the existing one. **In order for your organization to be successful there has to be a need for it.** To put it simply, if there is an organization fulfilling that need already, do not try to compete. Help them in their efforts.

Who is this organization going to benefit?

The last step in defining your organization is determining who the organization is going to benefit. This step in developing your organization is not as in-depth as the membership recruitment step, which is discussed in Step 4: Membership Recruitment. However, you need to get an idea of who this organization is going to benefit on campus before you can even begin recruiting. If you are the only beneficiary from this group's purpose, then there really is no need for the organization. **To maximize success, your organization needs to affect more people than just yourself.** Be open to as many people as possible. Try to broaden your purpose and member specifications so that a wide range of people will benefit from your mission. As stated earlier, an organization needs to have a clear and concise mission. However, do not broaden your mission to the point where it changes its focus. Just be sure that your organization's purpose is going to benefit as many people as possible. For example, it is acceptable to have an organization that is gender specific or has goals towards a particular sexual orientation or race. However, try to broaden your mission within these specifications. If you want to start a group to help women because you are a young woman who has suffered from sexism, do not name your group the "Women's Group Against Sexism." Instead title it the "Woman's Group Against Oppression" and make anti-sexism part of your mission statement along with other purposes. If you do not, a woman suffering from other issues will perhaps think the group is not for her. If your group is already

6

established, then re-analyze who your organization is trying to benefit and make changes if necessary.

ESTABLISH AN ORGANIZATIONAL STRUCTURE

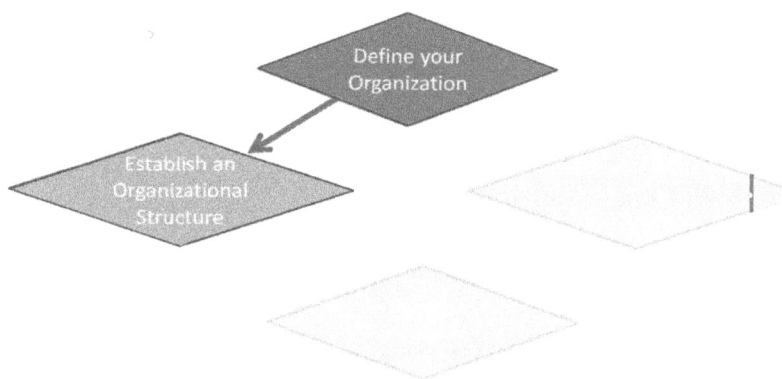

Now, that the organization's purpose has been defined, it is time to ask a question. *Who is going to help fulfill that purpose?* It is impossible for one person to run a successful organization. The leader has to be willing to listen and take direction from other members. However, you still have to maintain control of the organization in order to keep your vision intact. So how do you establish an organizational structure that allows everyone to have a say, but you maintain control? This is a two step process.

(1) Establish a leadership structure that calls for personal responsibility and a division of duties.

(2) Establish a cooperative relationship between the leadership and the membership, so that the ideas and needs of your membership are addressed.

The following are recommendations on how to accomplish these two steps. These are not the only ways to set up your organizational structure, but they have proven to work time and time again within many different student organizations. These steps can be followed whether you are starting an organization or leading an existing one.

Leadership Structure – "The Core 4"

A well organized and clearly defined leadership structure is what makes a solid organization. The easiest way to begin defining your leadership structure is by starting with a base to which everyone can relate. This base is your executive board, or as we like to call it, the *Core 4*. The Core 4 consists of your President, Vice President, Treasurer, and Secretary. This is a structure with which everyone is familiar and is common in most student organizations. The reason why it is so prevalent is because it works! It clearly sets up a chain of command and makes it easy to assign individual responsibilities. **A clear definition of everyone's role and duties is the most important thing in a leadership structure.** Everyone needs to know his/her accountability in an organization. The President is at the top of the ladder. He or she sets the overall vision, or mission, for the organization. The Vice President (VP) ensures that the goals established are being followed by the membership. The VP answers only to the President regarding membership decisions. The Treasurer is the next authority in line. The Treasurer is in full control of all financial business and ensures the chapter is reaching its financial goals. Finally, the Secretary is the center for all of the communication throughout the organization. He or she ensures that everyone in the group knows what is happening, and helps to maintain the focus of the group.

The Core 4 is shown in the diagram on the following page. The President sets the mission, symbolized by the umbrella. This umbrella is the vision or mission described in Step 1. Anything that falls outside of this umbrella is outside of the scope of the organization. The group decides on

SECTION 1:
ESTABLISH YOUR ORGANIZATION

the goals of the organization. The Vice President is in charge of passing on those duties to the membership. All financial needs to fulfill those duties are evaluated and approved by the Treasurer. The Secretary then gathers all that information made from the Core 4's decision making, and ensures that everyone clearly understands what the goals are and who is responsible for the duties at hand.

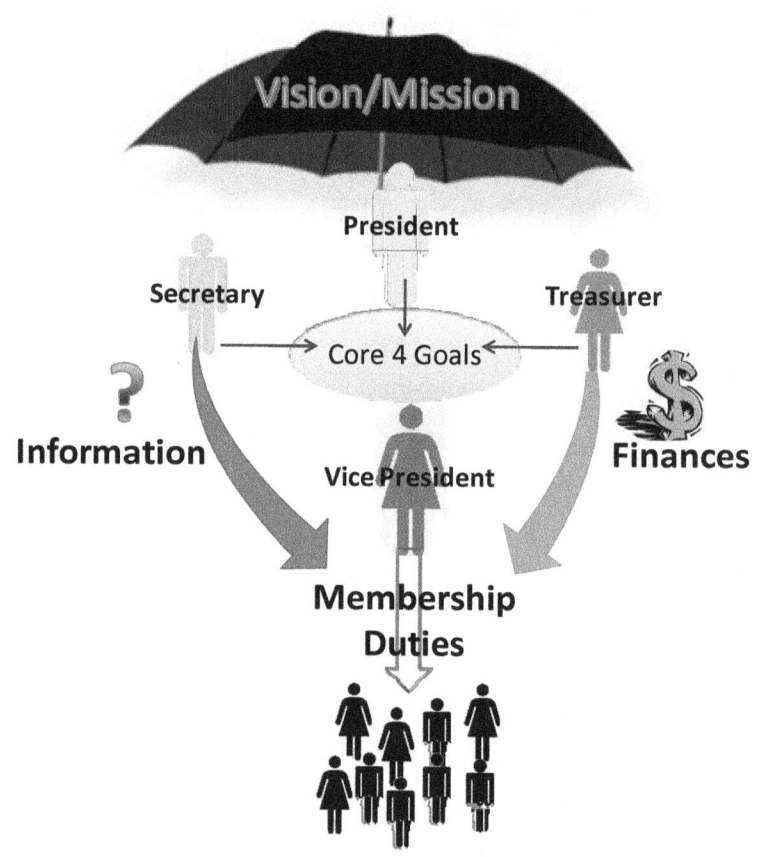

Below are some basic points that you can use to either create these positions or improve your existing ones. There are more responsibilities than listed, but these are the most essential powers and duties of each position in the Core 4:

President
- **Establishes the long-term vision of the organization and oversees development of short-term goals**
- Possesses the highest authority and has final say in all organizational decisions
- Is the only position that has authority over other members of the executive board (Core 4)
- Oversees and maintains outside relationships with individuals and groups (sponsors, other student organizations, advisors, alumni, etc.)
- Presides over all executive board meetings

Vice-President
- **Ensures that the short-term goals are being followed by the membership in order to fulfill the President's long term vision**
- Second in command under the president and takes control of the organization in his or her absence
- Has no control over the other executive members except in the president's absence
- Manages all membership information, actions, and responsibilities and has to verify actions with no one other than the President
- Manages all membership committees and groups
- Presides over all general membership meetings

Treasurer
- **Ensures that the organization has the funds necessary to carry out the defined goals and mission**

SECTION 1:
ESTABLISH YOUR ORGANIZATION

- Third in command in the absence of both the president and vice president

- Has no control over the other executive members except in the president's and vice-president's absences

- Oversees all financial decisions and has to verify actions with no one other than the president

- Generates fundraiser ideas in order to help the chapter financially support its goals

- Maintains records of off-campus bank account, on campus accounts, sponsor donations and any other funding for the organization

Secretary
- **Creates the center point of all organization information, and is responsible for the communication flow of the entire organization (i.e. announcements, meeting and event notices, etc.)**

- Last in command of the organization in the absence of the other members of the executive board

- Records all executive board and general meeting minutes

Membership Involvement

The next step in the process is to establish how the members are going to interact. A free expression of ideas from the members will help to make the organization succeed.

The best way to obtain the freedom of ideas and a sense of importance is to allow your members to have impact toward the fulfillment of the organization's goals. You as the leader have the vision; they as the members should have the ideas to fulfill the goals. For example, you are the the President of a volunteer organization that works with disabled children. Your mission is to help as many children as possible and be available for service any day of the week. You work with your executive board and set the obvious goal of increasing membership to accomplish this mission. Your VP will then work with the membership to get this goal accomplished. The members decide on a new program to increase the organization's membership. Letting them create it will allow the members to express their imagination and will prove they are as important to the organization as the leadership. This concept of goal setting will be discussed further in Step 3.

Another step in the process is to create a membership committee. A committee is a group of general members that have control over a certain program or issue. Committees are effective because they give structure to membership involvement. There are two effective types of committees. One is an *ad hock committee*. When a program or issue arises, allow members to volunteer and form an ad hock committee that either develops a program or solves an issue. Using the volunteer organization example stated above, the VP asks the group to develop a way to increase its membership. He or she could form a committee of members to generate the program idea. The other type of committee is a *structured committee*. A structured committee's role will never change. For example, you may have a Programs Committee that is in charge of putting on programs, or a Membership Committee whose sole purpose is to create ways to increase membership. These committees' roles will never change. When a member joins the organization they also join a committee. In order to give more power to the membership, there should be a member appointed as a chairperson to these committees who reports to the executive board on the committees' progress. This structure will guarantee effective decision making made by the membership body.

SET YOUR GOALS ACCORDING TO YOUR MISSION

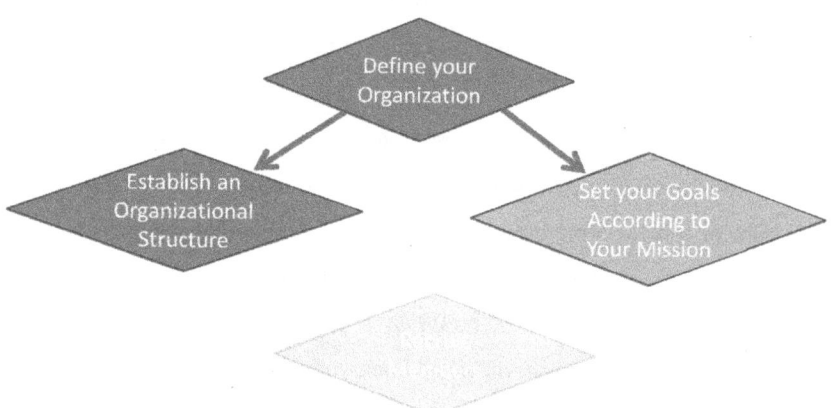

At this point you have defined your organization's mission and set up an organizational structure that will help fulfill this mission. Now, it is time to explain the steps that you and your organization will follow to fulfill that mission. These steps are your *organizational goals*. A mission statement answers the question "***What*** do we want to accomplish?", while goals answer the question "***How*** do we want to accomplish the mission?" By not addressing these questions, your organization will be unsuccessful. So, how does an organization begin to define the goals that will lead it to success?

There are a few things that a leader must do:

    (1) **Understand the differences between long term and short term goals**

    (2) **Associate a time frame to the goals**

(3) **Sculpt organizational programs around the goals**

(4) **Define "failure" for each goal and focus on continuous improvement**

The following discusses the direction on how to accomplish these four things. By incorporating these suggestions into your goal setting process, you will have guaranteed success.

Long Term vs. Short Term Goals

It is extremely important for you to divide your goals into short term and long term categories. **Short term goals are those that can be accomplished within one academic year.** They should be realistic and have a clear focus. This is not to say that your short term goals should not be challenging, but there is a need to be practical. For example, if your membership has been increasing by five members each year for the past few years, a realistic goal for the upcoming year may be an increase of eight to ten people. An increase of twenty however, may be too aggressive. The increase of twenty is an example of a long term goal. **Long term goals are those that are accomplished outside of one academic year.** They are realistic but require more work and time to accomplish. If you try to accomplish a long term goal in a short term time frame, you are setting the organization up for failure.

Associate a Time Frame for Your Goals

The best way to set your goals is to first look at your mission statement. Take your mission and create your long term goals with an appropriate time frame (i.e. greater than one year). Then plan your short term goals accordingly for the academic year. The amount of time to set for each goal is a decision for the organization's board (Core 4). Let's look at

SECTION 1:
ESTABLISH YOUR ORGANIZATION

Step 3

an example. You are the leader of an organization called "T.O.M.A.S." which stands for *Tutors of Math and Science*. Your group tutors high school students in math and science. Your mission is to "Decrease the number of high school students failing mathematics and science courses, and increase high school graduate interest in pursuing technical fields." Your organization's Core 4 decides that one of your goals would be to decrease the number of failing students in your city by 40%. This ties directly into the mission, but is not going to happen within one year. So, this should be a long term goal. Therefore, your long term goal is to decrease the number of failing students in your city by 40% **in four years**. Your short term goal **for the academic year** is to decrease the failing rate by 10%. If every year you decrease the failing rate by 10%, meeting your short term goals, you will ultimately reach your long term goals, fulfilling a portion of your mission.

Sculpt Organizational Programs Around These Goals

The next move is to assign programs that meet your goals. This ensures that all of your programs have a purpose and are helping the organization reach its goals. As mentioned earlier in Step 2, the members should help create ideas for the actual programs. You as the leader, however, must give them direction that ties these ideas to your goals and mission. Here is another example using T.O.M.A.S.. A short term goal is set to increase the number of high school students choosing technical undergraduate majors by 15%. This goal ties directly into the other part of the mission statement and seems realistic. The organization's Core 4 needs to decide on a program idea that helps accomplish this goal. Since you want to influence the students directly, you should come up with a fun and engaging program that calls for direct interaction between the high school students and your organization. You and your membership come up with ideas to teach the students about math and science. One idea is to have the students build remote controlled airplanes, which takes an entire weekend to complete. One day is spent learning about how an airplane works. The next day consists of using that knowledge to build and fly the airplanes. This is a fun idea that ties to the mission, accomplishes your goals, and results from cooperation between the leadership and membership. This is exactly what you want.

To help keep track of your goals, it is best to draw up an easy to follow document that lays out your mission, goals (short and long), time frames, and programs. Below is a table that would work for the T.O.M.A.S. group. Perhaps a similar format would work for your organization.

Mission: Decrease the number of high school students failing mathematics and science courses and increase high school graduate interest in pursuing technical fields.			
Type of Goal	*Goal*	*Time Frame*	*Program*
Long Term Goals	Decrease the number of failing students in your city by 40%	4 years	
Short Term Goals	Decrease the number of failing students in your city by 10%	1 year	Tutor children every day at various high schools
	Increase membership by 5%	1 year	Send out mail invitations to math and science majors about organization
	Incorporate 2 more local high schools to tutor	1/2 year	Send out mail descriptions to local high schools about the organization
Long Term Goals	Increase the number of students adopting technical undergrad majors by 60%	4 years	
Short Term Goals	Increase the number of students adopting technical undergrad majors next year by 15%	1 year	Weekend airplane design program
	Put on 15 programs with high school students that promote technical majors	1 year	See list of programs

Defining Failure and Continuous Improvement

What is failure? This is something that you and your leadership need to define for **EVERY** goal you set. Failing to meet a goal is not the end of the world. This just means you need to try harder. It is important to know when you have not met your goal. For some goals it's easy to define failure. For example, percentage goals, like the ones in the T.O.M.A.S.

example, are simple because if you do not meet that percentage...it is a failure. If you can set a number or percentage to your goal, then it makes the failure definition a lot simpler. Consequently, not all goals can be assigned a percentage. Goals like increasing membership participation or morale is something that cannot be seen directly. These are goals that definitely require membership input. You are going to have to work with your membership to determine if your plans for organizational improvement are working. **Even if you meet your percentages, the goal is still a failure if your membership is not happy with the outcome.** Remember that your members are the force that is helping to make your organization great. Their input as it relates to failure will help you to see the other side of the coin. In some cases their perspective may bring out a weakness that is not evident in the Core 4. So, the Core 4 and the membership need to establish what measure will be used to determine whether or not a goal is met. This measure is completely up to the organization, but needs to be easy to follow and an accurate representation of the goals outcome.

Lastly, every organization in order to be better needs a challenge. As the leader of the organization you need to strive for continuous improvement. Every year you have to want your organization to get better. If your goal of a five member increase was met easily, next year shoot for 10. If you raised $1000 last year, is it possible to raise $1500 this year? **The goals you set should always be in effort to improve the organization for both the long term and the short term.** Always strive to be better and continuously raise the bar. This means that you have to challenge each member of the Core 4. Every year increase the amount of money you want your Treasurer to raise. Ask what your Secretary's plans are to improve the communication. Discuss with your Vice President how membership morale can be increased. These are the challenges you should be giving to your leadership. If you challenge your leadership, you are in turn challenging yourself. You must improve **EVERY** academic year. If you do not, you will not be able to fulfill your mission; ultimately your organization will have no purpose.

RECRUIT MEMBERS

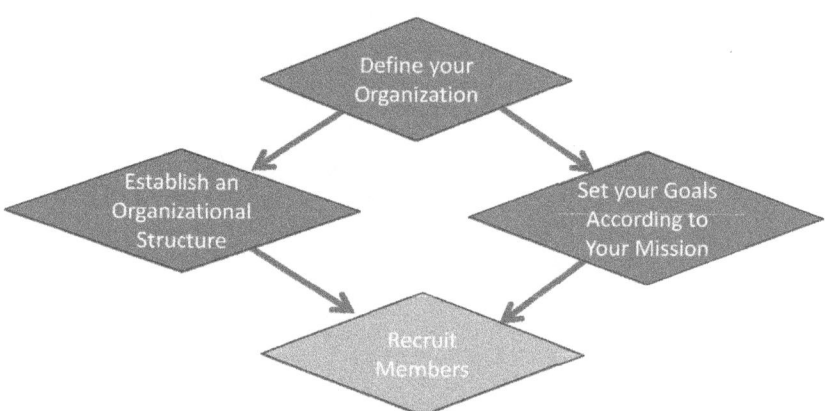

The last step in establishing your organization is *membership recruitment*. Membership recruitment is one of the most vital steps in creating an organization because members are the center of your club. As a student leader you need to understand that these individuals will build the organization up or take it down based on their involvement. It is imperative for every student leader to value his/her members because their ideas will ultimately lead to the organization's success.

Members should help your organization meet the goals that fulfill its mission. If a potential member is willing to help, then they are right for your organization. We will now discuss how to recruit members that best fit your mission and will help you accomplish your goals.

Numbers and Personality

The first part of recruiting is to set a number goal for your club. Have a number in mind of how many new students you want to attract to your organization. It is probably a safe bet to talk to twice the amount of people you want to recruit. For example, if you want 15 new members, then you probably need to talk to 30 or 40 students about your organization. Understand that not every student you talk to about your organization is going to join. Also, remember that there are other student organizations who are recruiting the same members you are.

When recruiting members it is important to understand their personality. As a student leader you need to determine what a potential member can bring to the table besides his/her immediate connection to the organization. This will give you a better understanding of what he/she can offer your group. A potential member who has an ability to create many ideas is an example of a specific trait of a **recruit's** personality. A talent like this can help your group to develop programs that garner attention from campus media. Even if these ideas are not specific to your vision, the person's ability to create new ideas could eventually help your club. The ideas would be new and may challenge you to think of your organization in new ways. This is the foresight and thinking process that a student leader needs when recruiting members

Meet and Greet

The next step in recruiting members is knowing where to get them, and how to attract them. Universities usually have a "Meet and Greet" night for students and student organizations at the beginning of the school year. This is the perfect opportunity to show off your club. Be prepared to talk about your organization and explain its benefits. You need to tell the students what your organization can do to help them. Prepare for these events as you would a job interview. Students are the interviewers and are going to want to know why they should choose your organization over another. Some benefits to tell potential members about are scholarships, volunteer opportunities, networking, traveling, raising money for charity, and leadership opportunities.

If you are a new leader of an established organization it may be a good idea to host a formal "Meet and Greet". This is an organization's meeting between members and recruits. It is an opportunity to make a huge impression on these recruits. Allow your current successful members to speak about the opportunities that your organization has offered and how it helps them in their college experience. The experiences that your current members share with potential members are a great help when recruiting. This third party exposure gives you and your organization credibility.

Your first initial "Meet and Greet" should be about the reasoning behind the organization. You should tell your potential members about the organization's goals and expectations. If you are starting an organization, a great idea is to have an event with food or something casual like a movie night. College students love food and anything that is free. This informal setting gives potential recruits an opportunity to hear what your organization is about. They will be able to talk to you and ask more personal questions about the organization. These meetings should leave you with a good number of new members that will add value to your organization.

Attract Members

If your organization has scholarships to give away, you should promote them heavily. Most college students are always looking for extra financial aid. Scholarships will be a main attention getter when recruiting members. A plus for any organization is that some scholarship programs require students to serve a certain amount of volunteer hours. Informing potential members that your club has volunteer opportunities may increase your chances in recruiting them.

Does your organization have conferences or large scale events? Pitching to potential members that they will have an opportunity to travel and network across the country is a great recruitment tool. Finally, remind the potential members that with all these opportunities you encourage them to become a future leader of the organization. The best way to make this relevant to the recruit is to tell him/her about future leadership opportunities that will benefit them in the future. For example, businesses are looking for people with leadership experience. Being a leader of an organization could potentially help that member land a future internship or job. This will show the member that you have their best interests in mind; your club can open doors of opportunities for him/her.

Uncomfortable Recruiting

Do not be afraid to step out of your comfort zone when recruiting members. Are you in class with someone who has similar interests as you? Ask if he/she has heard of your organization. Talk about the benefits of it. Invite new recruits to a meeting and get some feedback after the meeting.

If you take a bus or train to school with students, be sure to talk about your organization during those times. There will be ample opportunities on the bus to meet possible members. Talk to students to find their interests and see if their skills and abilities can help better your organization. Remember from Step 1 that diversity is essential and passion is a necessity when looking at potential members.

SECTION 1:
ESTABLISH YOUR ORGANIZATION

Step 4

If you are becoming a first time student leader, be sure to talk to alumni of your organization or other student leaders to see what ideas they have used to recruit members. The alumni and leaders are great resources.

It takes effort to recruit good quality members to your club. However, the work will come easy if you are able to embody your organization's mission. As the leader, your current and potential membership will look to your guidance and actions in order to understand the purpose of the organization. If you can stand tall and maximize every opportunity delivered to your organization, members will follow. When you present or speak about your club, be proud of it. Speak with confidence. This creates the perception among your members and recruits that **YOU** are the organization. This passion can bring you members that share your mission.

Section 2 – Strengthening your Organization: Building Unity, Maintaining Order, Retaining Membership, and Promoting a Positive Image.

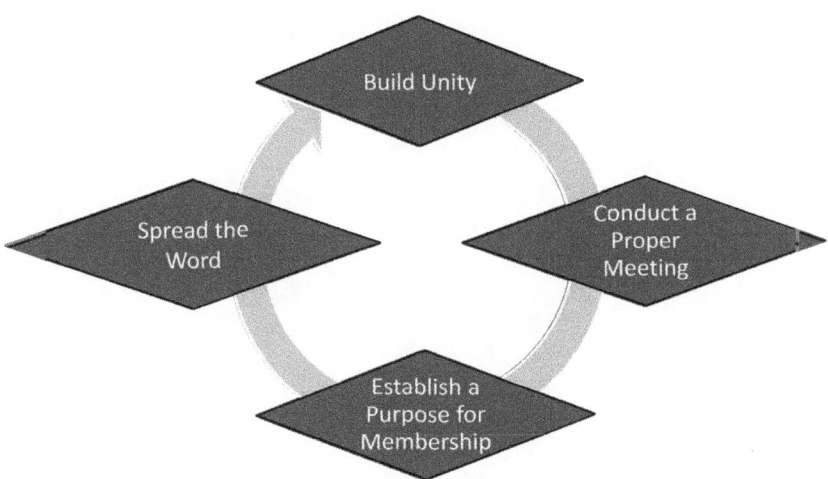

BUILD UNITY

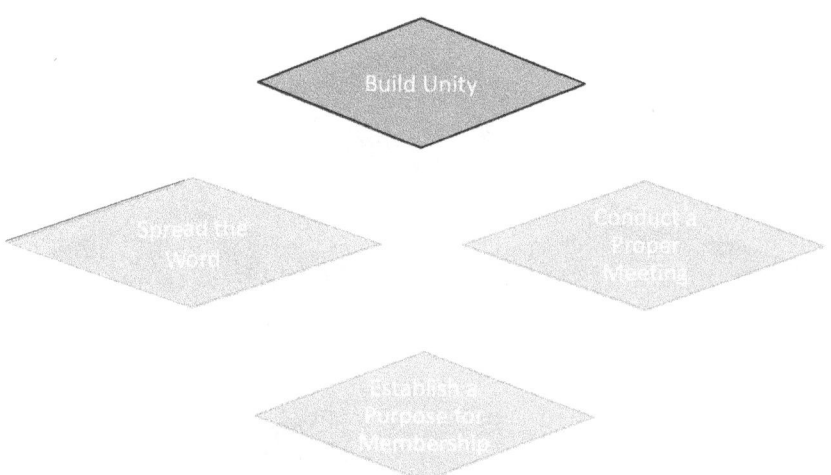

Now that you have completed the early steps of developing your organization and creating a foundation of success, it is time to build unity within the organization. Unity and team building often help in retaining good members. Just like a company needs good employees, an organization needs good members. It is up to the leadership to keep these members. Remember, members are the most important element of your group. By retaining them and their talents, your organization will experience growth and exposure.

In any sport it is important to have teamwork. A team can only function if it is working in harmony. That is how the San Antonio Spurs won 4 NBA Championships and the Chicago Bulls won 6 NBA

Championships. The following quote does a great job of describing the importance of teamwork:

> Jordan believed in Steve Kerr tonight, just as he did in John Paxton in the 1993 finals. With 10 seconds remaining and Game 6 tied, Jordan knifed between a double team and saw Steve Kerr standing a few steps behind the free throw line, and he flicked him the ball. The reserve guard knocked down a 17-foot jump shot with five seconds remaining and no time on the shot clock, a perfect swish that lifted the Bulls to an electric 90-86 victory over the Utah Jazz before a delirious throng at the United Center.[2]

Teams win championships because they play together and believe in each other. Each member performs his/her role to the best of his/her ability. In order to win championships the individual members have to trust each other and build unity. Trust and unity are important for your organization. Your members will have to embody the organization's mission and vision. In order to accomplish that the members must trust each other and work in harmony. As the leader you must build this inner trust and unity between members. The next sections of this chapter will discuss some techniques that will help to turn your group into a championship organization!!

Teambuilding

Every team starts at square one. Before the Spurs and Bulls won championships they started building unity in training camp. One way to build unity within your organization is to attend a teambuilding retreat. Consider these retreats "training camps" for your organization. This retreat

---

[2] Mike Wise. "A fistful of Rings: Bulls Grab Fifth Title of the 90's." *New York Times* (6.14.07)

SECTION 2:
STRENGTHEN YOUR ORGANIZATION

can also be used for you and your organization to focus on goal setting, brainstorming, and event planning. Retreats prepare you and your members to trust each other through various exercises, similar to a training camp. Though this may not sound exciting, you will see the benefits in the future when your members work on programs together throughout the academic year. During the school year, the members of your organization will work through problems on their own, and collectively develop ideas that will further the success and growth of your organization. In order to organize your retreat, you should talk to your Student Life Office or National Affiliate. If not, you should talk to your advisor and see what advice he/she may have on setting up a team building retreat for your organization. If your budget is not big enough to incorporate one, do not worry. There are other ways to build camaraderie within your organization.

Another way to build a strong team is to hire an individual to speak to your organization about teambuilding. Or you can have a university faculty or staff member speak about the subject. In any case, this individual should be skilled in teambuilding activities. These activities could consist of members speaking about their individual weaknesses, or discussing the future successes that they hope to accomplish with your organization. All of these activities encourage members to trust each other.

The final way to build team unity is to develop team building exercises on your own. One of the most common ways to test your organization's unity is by participating in a team sport. For example, does your school have intramural programs? Enroll your organization in one of these activities, and integrate the lessons you learn from the sport in your meetings. Now intramural sports are not the only team building exercise. You may want to talk to your Resident Advisor or your Campus Life Office to get more advice on team building exercises.

BUILD UNITY

Unity

Every championship organization has its players who all have roles to fill. By every player performing his or her role, the team is able to move as one. The best way to build unity among your membership is to empower them. Place your members in leadership roles like the chair of a committee, or head of volunteer activities. By creating these roles and giving members responsibility, they have a vested interest in the organization's success. Their role or department depends on their decision making ability. When considering members' ideas, understand that all final decisions about any activity must go through the Core 4. Making leaders out of your membership builds unity. This takes a great amount of trust from a student leader, because you are forced to believe in the ideas and abilities of your members. On the other side, showing that you support their decisions and hoping that their ideas will provide success to the organization, will help members trust you. As the leader of your organization, you should also listen to the members that are not in a position of power. These individuals are just as important as those members that have leadership roles. The ability to listen and implement your members' ideas will show that you are a leader that understands that you cannot create a successful organization alone. It makes the members feel valued and that is what it takes to build a championship organization. In order to continue to develop unity within your organization you must have fun. After your first meeting, start building unity by creating a "Get Together Night". This night could happen once a month or once every two months and is just for members of your organization. It could be a night where the whole group goes to the movies or to an amusement park. Since a college student's funds are limited, maybe a potluck and renting some movies to be played at a member's apartment would be a great idea as well. As the leader this is a great opportunity for your members to see the human side of you: they have seen

Step 5

you as the leader of the organization, but now it is time to relax. Enjoy the companionship that this night offers. It helps the members gain a better understanding of who you are as a person. Do your best to not mention organizational work. If you are a shy person, do not fear this opportunity to socialize. It will become easier the more you do it. This event also provides you with an opportunity to get to understand your members too. You can find their passion and understand what motivates them. By doing this you establish a connection with your members; they will in turn have a strong relationship with your organization.

Sharing

Sharing is one of the biggest traits that a championship organization has. When the Bulls won their championships, Michael Jordan thanked and praised his teammates for their efforts. Understand that as a leader it is important for you to share your success with members. By acknowledging your member's efforts and accomplishments you help your organization grow and be successful. For example, did one of your members plan a successful program? During the meeting, take time to thank that individual for his/her hard work and dedication. Rest assured that a little gratitude goes a long way, and it is important for a student leader to show it!

A great idea in regards to membership recognition is to have a "Member of the Month" program. Set aside a little money in the budget to take a member out to lunch to celebrate his/her efforts. Another idea is to have a giveaway of a $20 gift card to a local grocery or department store. These small gifts go a long way in showing the appreciation you have for your members' efforts. Has your organization been working extremely hard? Bring in some donuts or pizzas for the group during a meeting. This is one small way to show your gratitude for your members' hard work.

These acts will be implanted in the members' minds and may help them to continue to participate in your organization.

Support

The final trait that a championship organization has is support. One of the biggest influences in a member's teamwork attitude is the leader's actions. For example, you may have a member that is involved with another student organization, such as theater. Have you thought about attending a performance to show your support for that student? It is important for you as a student leader to take time out of your schedule to support your members in their other activities. It is a great way to show that you care and are interested in what they do outside of your organization.
Finally, the best way to promote unity and teambuilding within your organization is to be a servant leader. What is a servant leader? A servant leader is an individual that is not afraid to get his/her hands dirty; doing whatever it takes to help a member succeed. If a member is in charge of a volunteer activity and asks for your help, be a team member and be of service. You are empowering them, and showing that you are willing to help. It will benefit you and your organization greatly in the long run.

CONDUCT A PROPER MEETING

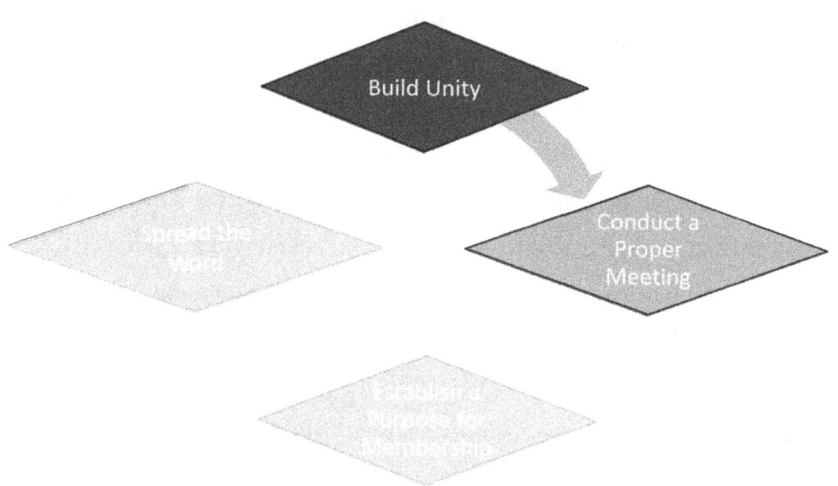

At this point, you have created an organizational structure, recruited members and built unity among the group. It is time to start putting your plans into action. In order to do this, your organization needs to meet frequently to follow through with the goals set by the Core 4. Nearly all organizations have some form of group meeting. Usually these are where major decisions are made and where the order and maturity of your organization is defined. Since meetings are so important, you as a leader have to understand how to structure and run a meeting effectively. This chapter will give the necessary preparation process to ensure that your meetings are effective and you are getting the most out of your members' time.

Before Any Meeting

Regardless of what type of meeting (Core 4 meeting, general body meeting, etc.) there are two main questions that a leader must ask before holding it. **What is the purpose of this meeting?** and **How should the meeting be structured?** If the answers to these questions are not clear to you, your meetings may turn out to be unsuccessful, in turn hurting your organization's cause. The first question about purpose is the most important question of all. As stated a few times already, **before every meeting make sure that there is a purpose and that you are not meeting just to meet**. Meeting out of tradition with no purpose wastes your Core 4's time, your members' time, and your time. The first question could also read, *"What are you trying to accomplish from this meeting?"* The answer to this question will differ depending on which type of meeting you are holding, but you need to have an understanding of what you hope to accomplish from this meeting. If there is not anything that needs to get accomplished, then do not hold a meeting!

Now, the second question about structure is extremely important as well because even with a defined purpose, a meeting cannot run without structure. A well-structured meeting has five key elements: **a clear agenda, defined order or tone, consistent time, suitable location, and appropriate frequency**. These five elements are going to be different for each type of meeting, but they all need to exist. In the following sections are the two types of meetings - Core 4 and general body (membership) - and how to define the purpose for these meetings and structure them for success.

SECTION 2:
STRENGTHEN YOUR ORGANIZATION

Core 4 Meetings

The Core 4 meetings are obviously the ones that consist of your elected board (President, Vice President, Treasurer and Secretary). However, they can also include any committee chairpersons. These meetings are held by the President and are focused on setting the goals that fulfill your organization's mission. Think of these meetings as almost a type of strategy meeting. All of you need to strategize how you want to fulfill your mission. It is imperative that you have these additional meetings outside of your general membership meetings to make sure everyone is working as a unit and is ready to lead. So, how do you run a Core 4 meeting? Apply the earlier questions to find out how.

What is the purpose of this meeting?

The purpose of every board meeting is to ensure that the organization is fulfilling its mission. At the very beginning of the academic year, the purpose of your meetings will be easy to see, because you will be defining your goals for the year. Once you have set all your goals however, some inexperienced organizations see no need for an elected board meeting and stop having them. To be frank, there should always be a reason for an elected board meeting. This may confuse you because earlier it was stated "never meet just to meet." But for the Core 4, there should always be things to plan and issues to resolve. Once you have planned your goals for the year, you will need to have meetings on the progress of those goals. Also, do not be afraid to start planning goals for the next academic year. Any issues that involve the membership, such as conflict or drop in morale, needs to be addressed at this meeting as well. You may have a meeting just resolving an intense issue. This may not be setting goals, but it is equally as important. You cannot fulfill your mission if the membership is not functioning properly. So, even though the purpose of the Core 4 meetings seems simple, it has a wide range of topics and is extremely important.

How should the meeting be structured?

Let's look at the five key elements of meeting structure for this meeting.

1. Clear Agenda

The foundation of a well-run meeting is a well-formed agenda. An agenda is an outline of your thought process that will guide the meeting. A well-written agenda is imperative in a Core 4 meeting, even more important than in a general membership meeting. This is because in a board meeting you are handling the vision of the organization and need to have well thought out logic to back up your decisions. Make sure that your agendas for each meeting are attacking the most current issues. Also, make sure you give time in your agendas to allow for feedback from your board. The agenda guidelines are given in the example section. Make sure you review them and follow them every time you write an agenda for your meeting.

2. Tone

Tone is different in every type of meeting. What is meant by tone is the atmosphere of the meeting. How are people conducting themselves? In a Core 4 meeting, there needs to be order and a certain amount of professionalism. This is because, as stated many times, this is the meeting where the important decisions are made. In order to manage these decisions and people's feelings, you need to have a business tone to your meetings. This may be slightly different than your general body meetings. ALL YOUR MEETINGS NEED TO BE RESPECTFUL, but your membership meetings can be fun and engaging at times which will require a different

SECTION 2:
STRENGTHEN YOUR ORGANIZATION

tone. The Core 4 frankly needs to "be about the business." Make sure your actions, mannerisms and agendas reflect this need.

3. **Consistent Time**

This means that **your meetings need to be on the same day and at the same time.** Never fluctuate your Core 4 meeting times. This places a sense of importance on your meetings. Remember, the Core 4 positions are elected positions. There needs to be a sense of responsibility within them. There should be a lot less flexibility here than it would be with membership meetings. This may mean disciplinary action if tardiness is consistent, but this also means making sure that your time and location works for everyone on the board.

4. **Suitable Location**

Try to reserve something small and quiet so that you can conduct business in the right manner. Have it in an area that promotes professionalism, that has a seating arrangement that allows everyone to be visible, and has some form of visual aid (white board, projector, etc.). If your school has a student organization center with a small meeting room, this would be perfect. If not, see if you can reserve a classroom or something this size. Try to stay away from people's homes if possible, and never do any meetings in crowded areas like restaurants or other large gathering places.

5. **Appropriate Frequency**

The days and times you have your Core 4 meetings are decided by you and your board. However, there is always a question of how often you need to meet. **Core 4 meetings should occur twice as much as membership meetings**. If the general body meets once a month, your board needs to meet twice a month. If the members meet every two weeks, you need to meet with your board every week. Unless there are extenuating circumstances, like a large event or important fundraiser, **you should never have to meet more than once a week**. Also, try to meet close to your general body meeting days. This way you can plan out your general meetings and make sure everything is on track. If you follow these guidelines, you will have successful Core 4 meetings.

General Body Meetings

As a student leader it is important to distribute information to your members. The best way to do this is through a general body meeting. General body meetings are the link between the membership and Core 4. During general body meetings topics discussed during Core 4 meetings should not be revealed. The only time topics should be revealed is if the President and Vice President agree that information from a Core 4 meeting needs to be discussed to the membership.

What is the purpose of this meeting?

During this time you will talk about upcoming programs, events, and activities. Items that may be discussed during this time are topics that were brought up during the Core 4 meeting. This meeting is usually held by the Vice President of an organization. Similar to the Core 4 meetings, the goal is to take care of business. However, the meetings will not be the same depending on the atmosphere the student leader wishes to set.

SECTION 2:
STRENGTHEN YOUR ORGANIZATION

How should the meeting be structured?

Let us look at the five key elements of meeting structure for this meeting.

1. Clear Agenda

As stated earlier, it is important for a student leader to have an agenda for the meetings. An agenda is the outline of topics that will be discussed during a meeting. It should be prepared at least two days before a meeting. This gives you time to adjust and look over your agenda just in case you may have to rearrange topics. An agenda keeps track of discussion items, and shows the membership that you take meetings seriously. Address each discussion point in order to keep the group moving forward.

2. Tone

General body meetings are much different than Core 4 meetings in regards to tone. The tone of a Core 4 meeting requires the attention and focus of the group. The Core 4 team goes over important items that will determine the success of the organization. The general body meetings are important, but the meeting's tone does not require the intense attention as a Core 4 meeting. As the student leader in charge of general body meetings you have to make them engaging. You do not have to reinvent the wheel. Ask past student leaders what they did during meetings to keep the membership excited and interested. An example of an engaging meeting for a professional organization is to conduct a resume workshop. These workshops help members prepare for "Corporate America." Schedule a general meeting that discusses this. Some items on your agenda may have to be discussed at a later date in order to make this happen.

One example of an enticing and engaging meeting involves current events. Is there an issue on campus that is gaining attention? Have a meeting to discuss the issue, and get a measure of your member's feelings about a relative issue, such as a decrease in public funding. It greatly affects some members by decreasing scholarship availability for them. Is there an event in the news or in the community that your group should address? Have a meeting talking about the event. This keeps members engaged and challenges them to participate. Whatever the issue is, be sure to talk about it. Create a presentation that goes over the issue. During the presentation lay out all the facts of the matter, question your members, and get their perspective on the topic at hand.

A final example of having an engaging meeting involves classes. Do your members get confused about scheduling classes? Have a general meeting that talks about the ins and outs of scheduling classes so members can graduate on time. Bring in a seasoned professor to talk about the classes students can take in order to use their money efficiently. If you have students with different majors, locate professors that are in member's field so they can talk about classes these students should be taking.

Students in your organization have so much happening that it is difficult at times to garner their attention. However, you have a task at hand and must deliver the information to the group. It is acceptable to have a meeting where the members exchange ideas and discussion points, but do not let this get out of hand. Be sure to take control of your meeting by asking for respect from the group. State that you wish to get them out as early as possible, but the only way to do this is if they cooperate and listen.

3. **Consistent Time**

As mentioned earlier, especially for membership meetings, make sure that you have a set time and day that you are meeting. Members have so much happening and should not be burdened with inconsistent scheduling. The only time a meeting should be changed is for an emergency. Otherwise, meetings should be planned in advance, and members should be notified immediately.

4. **Suitable Location**

Locations of meetings are extremely important. If you have a large group and are in a cramped space, you can expect a lot of complaints that will disrupt your meeting. Make sure to have a set room or space where your group can meet in comfort. In addition, be sure the room has the necessary tools/items (computer, projector, desks, etc.) you need in order to provide information to the members. If you have a small group, a classroom setting is fine. However, make sure that the setting has the essential items you need to properly run your meeting.

5. **Appropriate Frequency**

Finally, make sure that you are having meetings at least once a week or bi-weekly on the same day, at the same time. Information flows so fast these days that you need to keep the group apprised of upcoming programs and events. This helps to keep your organization moving forward without missing a step. Also, if you do not need a meeting, cancel it. Members will respect you for just saying that there is nothing to cover. Do not waste your member's time by holding unnecessary meetings. If the information can wait, let it wait.

Conclusion

Meetings are the most important resource for you and your organization to share information. It is important to have this face to face interaction with the members. It helps to keep everyone updated on what is occurring throughout the organization. These membership meetings also help to build rapport and unity within your group. As the student leader, Core 4 and membership meetings help you to determine which people in your group are dedicated to the mission and vision of the organization. Their attendance, participation, and interaction will show you if they are ready to become future leaders of the organization.

ESTABLISH A PURPOSE FOR MEMBERSHIP

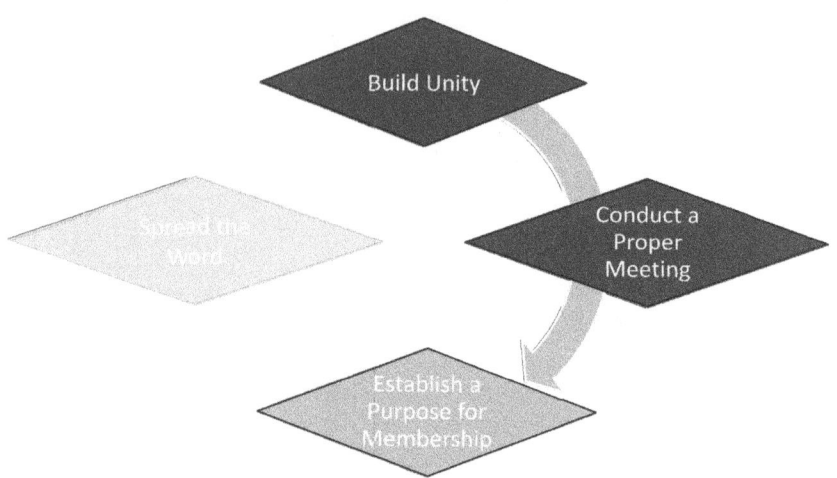

As stated in Step 4, the members of an organization are pivotal elements of its success. Each member has the potential to lead an organization, provide great programming ideas, and actively participate in every meeting. Therefore, it is the responsibility of the leadership to keep the members engaged and give them a reason to attend meetings. While the classroom develops a member's academic skills, a student organization should develop the remaining skills that will prepare them for their future. It is imperative that an organization's members want to be a part of the organization and feel like they are learning something from every activity. *This is one of the most essential points of this book and an important aspect*

of strengthening the organization. This chapter will further discuss membership involvement and establishing a high morale among members.

New Members

After you have attracted new people to attend your meetings, your job is not done. You must make sure they return. Extra caution should be taken when you have new members attend. They need to know information about your organization. What you do in that meeting is going to determine whether or not that person attends again. Try to think of this as a first date or an interview. Unless you put forth your best effort to impress this person, you most likely will not have him/her return for another meeting. After the meeting is over, the leadership should take the person aside and inform this person of the key aspects of the organization: the mission, vision, and key events planned. It is important to answer any of his/her questions. If after gaining all the information, they are not comfortable returning and feel like the organization is not a good fit, then that is perfectly fine. Just make sure that you as the leader did everything to make that person return.

Meeting Substance

A sign of a successful organization is the ability to have members leave a meeting knowing they gained some important information. Remember to always have members attend to your meetings happy to be there and leave with the same amount of enthusiasm. This is a good indication that they enjoy being in your organization and will attend the next meeting. Make sure that each meeting is structured so that members are getting important information about the status of the organization and upcoming events. Also, become creative with information that is covered in meetings. Possibly discuss current events related to your organization and have a discussion among everyone. For example, if you were in the "I Love Cars" club, then you would want to bring up the latest trends in the automotive industry and facilitate a discussion on that. Try to find things that are potential developmental learning experiences. The topic of current and other details on how to run efficient meetings was described in Step 6.

Member Roles and Responsibilities

Another thing to keep in mind regarding membership retention is *what their role is in the organization*. Are the members just soldiers that carry out your orders? Do they have any say in the decision making? Your organization was created to do something, and your members are an important part of what you plan on doing. It was stressed in Step 2 that members need to feel that they have an active role in the organization. If this occurs, they have honest reasons to return to your meetings and participate in program planning and execution. You must always keep in mind that this is something that they are electing to do in their own free time; time they could be spending doing other activities. They do not **have** to show up to each meeting. In order to keep members interested, create sub-committees, as suggested in Step 2, so that they can plan and execute programs and events. This allows them to take ownership over something in the organization, giving them a greater feeling that they are contributing to its success. If your group is not large enough to create sub-committees, then try to find a way to give members greater roles. Using the "I Love Cars" club scenario, you could create a sub-committee that would research all General Motors products. Then you could have members in that committee be in charge of researching specific brands such as GMC, Chevrolet, etc. and reporting back to the group on any new information they have found. This makes them feel as though they are contributing something to the organization.

Keep it Positive

A positive attitude that resonates throughout an organization makes members want to return each week. Starting from the top, the leadership of an organization must constantly be excited about all aspects of his/her organization. If he/she is not, then it is very difficult for members to be excited and interested. There must be a bright and positive attitude shown in each element of the organization. This helps members decide to attend and be active in your organization. Also, members will pass along this excitement to their friends; new members may join because of this exhilarating passion. It is up to the leadership to find ways to motivate and keep the organization going in the right direction.

Any negative situations that arise must be toned down so that membership morale never declines. As the leader, you need to be honest with your members during the negative times, but you need to stand firm and have a positive outlook on the situation. If you are positive and steadfast during the negative times, the membership will gain respect for your decision making ability and morale will increase.

Flexibility

At critical times during a school semester you may need to be more flexible in your schedule. If key times of the semester (midterms or finals) are approaching, perhaps you should cancel a meeting or move around events. When you decide to move events or meetings be sure to include the membership in the decision. They may come up with a better event or meeting alternative. This flexibility and understanding shows that the organization cares about its members and knows the importance that they play in its success. Also, you need to be aware of an individual member's morale. This emotional shift could have nothing to do with the organization. As the school year progresses and as things happen in their personal lives, members tend to wear out and become disengaged. If you notice that a particular member is having a rough time with something, inquire about it and show that you care about his/her welfare. This definitely adds to a member wanting to be a part of your organization.

SPREAD THE WORD: POSITIVE PROMOTION AND ADVERTISING

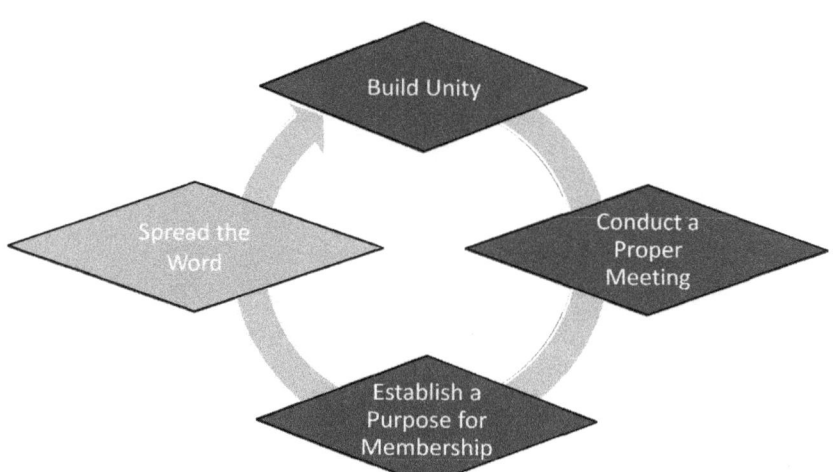

So far, we have established the ground rules for creating and maintaining a strong organization. You should now know how to run a meeting and how to recruit and maintain members. It is now time to learn how to promote your organization. Promoting is a key element to successful campus organizations. With today's technology there are many ways to inform others about your organization. This chapter will discuss the importance of promoting/advertising your organization and the different methods of doing it. We will also discuss briefly the ethical decisions involved in promoting your organization and how those decisions are essential to your organization's success.

Importance of Promotion and Advertising

Advertising your organization is essential to your growth and success. As a student leader, you want to make sure that the group is seen in a positive way. Promoting your organization can also enhance your campus image. Depending on the positive publicity, it could help your organization gain notoriety and members. When promoting your group, make sure that you use every campus resource available: internet, campus radio stations, campus calendars, and fliers. Just as a company advertises on TV, radio, and the Internet when it launches a new product, you will have to use campus media to let students know about your organization and the programs that you are planning.

Ways of Promoting and Advertising: Pt.1

Next, you will have to allocate funds for advertising / promotion in your budget (see Step 9 for Budgeting). The most cost effective way to advertise is through word of mouth and fliers. Student organizations, many times, have very limited funds. These two avenues give you the most "bang for your buck". Word of mouth and fliers are the foundation of advertising for many student organizations. These mediums are easy to use and allow the organization to get their word out.

There are three important aspects when promoting with fliers. Have the name of your organization prominently displayed. This allows students to know who is sponsoring the program. Whenever you promote, the most valuable thing you have is the name and image of your organization. Think about McDonalds for instance. The symbol of the Golden Arches is identifiable whether you are in America or Japan. You want to have this type of recognition for your organization; the best way to start is through fliers. The second thing you need is the date and time of your organization's event. This information is valuable because it tells the students when, where, and why you are having this event. This may sound basic, but these things are the building blocks for promoting your organization effectively. Finally, you need to make sure that your flier is creative enough to stand out among other fliers. There are many student organizations on your campus. You want to make your group's fliers stand out by utilizing creative colors or images. You want to be recognizable and build your organization's image with your advertising. Through creative promoting you are hoping to build the curiosity of students, so that they will want to attend your meeting or program. In college, with so many activities (class, homework, and social events) it is very difficult to gain the attention of students. There is also fierce competition to get attendees to campus events, as multiple organizations tend to have programs occurring on the same day. If an organization has a great program and they can get the campus talking about it, students will be more inclined to go to that organization's next event. Fliers should be used to get the word out; however it should not be the only method implemented to promote your event. Examples of good and bad fliers are located in the appendix.

Word of mouth gives you a direct connection with possible attendees to your event. It also gives you the power to state your message the way you want. If you spin your event the right way, it may build a student's interest and get him/her to come to your event. Interact with people all day in class. Don't be afraid to make an announcement about your event at the end of a class. By delivering your message personally, it allows an attendee to put a face to the organization and program. It also lets you know if your advertising methods are working. Students will let you know if they have heard about your program or not. This feedback is invaluable because it allows you to make changes to your promoting based on the needs of the student. You will discover that word of mouth is a very powerful tool, especially when you have a third party talking about your event. When another person tells others about your event, it builds the interest of the students. They think that this person is not just a part of the organization, but he/she is really excited about this event. "I should go to find out what the excitement is about." When a student's thinking changes to this, your advertising has done its job!

Ways of Promoting and Advertising: Pt.2

The other mediums to consider when promoting your organization are radio, internet, and TV. These may be costly forms of media depending on your school. If they are free, you should definitely take advantage of them. For example, if your school has a TV station and offers free advertisement, post your events on it. It could be a static billboard, or you can develop a creative commercial. Does your campus have a student run radio station? This provides you a great opportunity to place a promoting message in front of students. Also, most schools have a calendar of events where you can post your programs or meetings. Promoting is all about building awareness and gaining attention. These different ways of advertising will help accomplish that. Finally, we cannot forget about the Internet. This is the quickest and easiest way to get your message to others. Does your student organization have a Facebook©, MySpace©, or other social networking profile? If not you should create one. Use it to send messages to other organizations about your event.

There are many avenues to spread the word about your group and events. However, as a student leader it is up to you to maximize these mediums. Conduct a survey after an event to find out which promoting avenues worked the best for getting those people to attend. You might discover that students listen to the radio more, or notice fliers, etc. This will tell you if you should shift some of your advertising budget from fliers to radio or vice versa. Do your best to promote the organization. Giving a survey to your event's attendees help to measure your advertising's effectiveness. Also, if you have a student organization center, be sure to attend the seminars on promoting to gain more experience.

Ethics and Advertising

When promoting and advertising an organization, student leaders need to embody good ethics. It is important for a leader of an organization to show him/her self in a positive light. Bad publicity can result from negative actions, sayings, or misinterpretations. As a campus leader you must choose your words and actions carefully. Consider your student leader role akin to being a celebrity or politician. Though you are not making a million dollars, or creating laws that will change America, you are under a microscope and are promoting your organization by your actions.

People are always looking at you when you are a student organization leader. You need to be aware of your surroundings and with whom you associate. These responsibilities all come with the territory of being a leader. For example, you are at a party and having a good time. The host is serving alcohol at this party. You are under age, and there are other people your age drinking. As a student leader you need to think twice about the decision to drink. If you do decide to drink and are caught, what does that mean to your organization? What type of message are you sending to your present members and your future members? This will be one of the many ethical situations you may face as a student leader.

Let us look at another scenario. You and a leader of another student organization are in a heated disagreement over a program. In order to win the argument you decide to spread a dirty secret about that organization. Maybe, that organization has done some scandalous deeds in the past, or you made up some false information about them. You decide to humiliate them by putting that information out to the campus public. In this scenario, you need to think of the outcome. What happens if you do something that is not particularly popular in the campus organization community, and an organization decides to spread a secret or slander about your organization? How would you feel? What would you do? All of this negative energy and promoting could have been spent coordinating an event or program for you and your organization.

Remember you are still promoting your organization when you spread the misinformation. If you did decide to spread rumors about another organization without cause, the leader of that organization might look at you differently. They may not co-program with your organization, or support any of your initiatives. Your credibility is non-existent due to the bad publicity that you are promoting. As a new student leader you do not want to have this scenario happen. A struggling student organization does not last long.

We have already stated that a very important aspect of a student organization is the membership. Now, they may not be in the spotlight like the student leader, but their actions do have an impact on the way the campus community views your organization. You cannot control the actions of members; you are not their mother or father. You can only advise the student on the ethical choices he/she will face. If a student's choice is harmful to your organization, you should seriously consider eliminating that student's membership. It may be a difficult decision at first, but it may need to be done. For example, your organization goes on a trip to a museum in Chicago. One member decides to not attend the museum and uses this time to do his/her own thing. This was not originally in the plans. As the leader you must make a decision to keep that member, or ask him/her to leave. If you allow them to stay, have some type of consequences for the individual's actions. You cannot have members doing their own thing if it is not a part of your planned trip. Yes, members can go off when there is free time. However, when you plan scheduled events for members to attend, they should be participating.

Conclusion

We have covered the basics of promotion and advertising. Remember to creatively develop your advertising. Make it stand out to gain the attention of students. Also, the most cost efficient way to advertise / promote is word of mouth and fliers. Finally, remember as a student leader you are under a microscope. The school administration, students, and other organizations are always looking at what you do. Make sure that you are making ethical decisions in order to promote your organization in the best light.

Section 3 - Maintaining Your Organization: Budgeting, Fundraising, Networking, and Developing New Officers

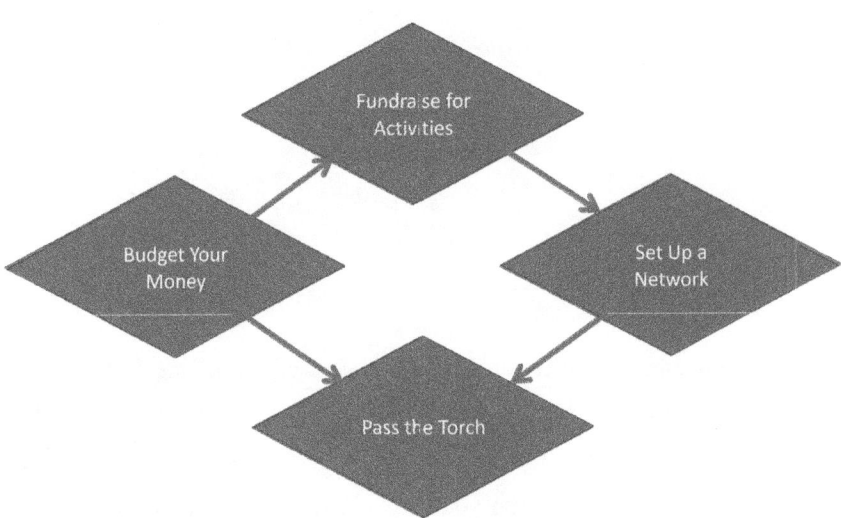

BUDGET YOUR MONEY

Creating a budget is a key component of organizing and attaining funds in an organization. Efficient organizations use a budget as a tool to organize their finances. The purpose of a budget is to have an idea of how much money you need to run your organization, and what to spend it on once you have it. Therefore, a budget is a formal way of looking at the finances for the next academic school year. Budgeting also answers the questions "How much money do I request in order to run all of my programs?" and "With the money our organization has, how should I spend it efficiently?" These questions lead to two reasons for creating a budget. These reasons are requesting funds from the university or external source, and determining how to allocate them. This chapter will further discuss these different reasons mentioned above, as well as how to make a budget, and who should create it for your organization.

Requesting Money

In terms of requesting funds, your budget will be used as an organized document that justifies whatever amount that your organization is requesting. If someone were to ask you why you are requesting a certain amount of money or for what it will be used, you can point to your budget and give answers. This adds to the credibility of your requests and makes you more likely to receive the amount you are requesting. In order to create a budget, you first need to know your plans for the upcoming academic year. At this point, your organization should have discussed goals and ideas for programs, because programs are one of the components for budgets. In the budget, you need to itemize and list ALL the things that will cost money. For example, if you are in the "I Love Video Games" organization and your organization wants to have a video game tournament, then you need to discuss the things that will cost money. This process can take some time as there are many variables. You need video games; either they can be purchased, or borrowed. If purchased, then it goes into the budget. The same goes for the console and any accessories. Also, if you want to use a big screen TV to show the games, then you need to consider the question "Do you need to rent the TV?" If so, then this needs to go into the budget. What about room rental? Do you need to rent a space to have the event or can you get it free from the university? This is the thought process that needs to occur for creating a budget. You need to dig deep into your programs and try to come up with figures associated with each item. That is why it is important to have your programs well thought, so that the budget process goes smoothly in order to answer the many logistical questions that will be asked. This is one of the reasons why you may want to have a group of people plan out and discuss the details of the programs. You will want to have many perspectives to plan the budget accordingly. Then, when the budget is being created, you can show details of what is needed and possibly cost associate, allowing the treasurer to put items in the budget in a timely manner.

Other than programs, you should also account for possible miscellaneous costs. If you are going to have meetings, then you need to account for how you want to advertise meetings. If you are going to just send emails out, you do not need any money. However, if you are going to hang fliers around campus, you may need money for advertising. Also, if you want to have food at your meetings, you may need to add food in your budget. These type of things start off as small additions, but they can add up. Therefore, it is very important to discuss and determine non-program related costs that may arise over the course of the academic year.

Money Allocation

As mentioned above, a budget also serves as a tool that allows you to properly allocate funds for your organization. If your organization already has a set number of dollars given to you by the university or another external source, then a budget will give you an idea of how to allocate efficiently. The difference is that you do not have to request funds since they are already given to you.

Depending on your organization, there are many ways to distribute these funds. One way is to create multiple levels to your budget, as a top-down approach. For example, the "I Love Video Games" club main goals are to play video games all the time, get more members, and have a video game tournament. You were allocated $1,500 for your organization to operate with for the academic year. So in your budget, you can start from the top. If you want $500 for tournaments, $500 for getting more members, and $500 for just video game playing and development, you can create "mini budgets" for each of these levels. Similar to money requests, you can discuss all the things that you would need for each of these levels. For example, if you want to discuss general video game playing and development, you would discuss the activities that are associated with this. Examples of these activities would be buying the latest games for each console you have, subscribing to magazines, etc... Then, you would list the costs associated with each task. The same would go for each of the higher level groups you created.

Budget Tweaking

In both uses of a budget, money request, and money allocation you will probably come to a point when the money you need is more, sometimes much more, than the money you will actually obtain. In money allocation, it is easier to know this because you know how much you have in the beginning. However, for requesting money, you will not really know how much you will get. In both cases, you will more than likely need to make cuts to your budget. This normally occurs because your organization is very optimistic about its goals and programs for the upcoming year. However, this is where you need a strong treasurer to bring you down to Earth. Your treasurer needs to be able to strongly say, "No, we can't do this because we don't have enough money." in many instances during budget cuts. Your organization at this point needs to look at the budget and decide the areas where money can be cut. In some cases, you may want to just take a specified dollar amount from each spot in your budget. Or, you may want to just cut out an entire program. This depends on your organization and the goals and programs that you set out for yourself at the beginning of the process. One thing to note is that you cannot leave the budget process unless the necessary cuts have been made. If you do, then you will come to a point where you will run out of money, and something you planned to do in your budget will not get done.

SECTION 3: MAINTAIN YOUR ORGANIZATION

Key Player

The treasurer is the main person that creates the budget and facilitates the discussion around it. Your organization needs to have a strong treasurer: someone who can think rationally and know what cuts need to be made and is not afraid to say "No." This is important as there will be many cases where you will need someone who can say, "No, we just can't do that" or "We just don't have the money for that." Also, you need a person who is highly detail-oriented when creating the budget and coming up with all possible costs. Another key attribute is someone with math skills. You do not want to come to a point where you cannot put on a program because your treasurer erred mathematically and you do not have enough money.

Also, try to get people other than the treasurer involved as you will be trying to generate ideas for what to put in the budget. You could have a conservative treasurer who only wants to do the bare necessities to put on programs. This could result in your programs not meeting the expectations of the people who originally created them. It would be best to schedule a special meeting to talk about the budget. The process to create it can be long, so do not try to fit it in a Core 4 meeting, where other things will be discussed. In terms of membership, you would only need those members who are part of the program planning process, as they can give you details on what is involved and any costs that may occur. In order to illustrate all the topics discussed in this chapter, an example of a budget is shown in the appendix.

FUNDRAISE FOR ACTIVITIES

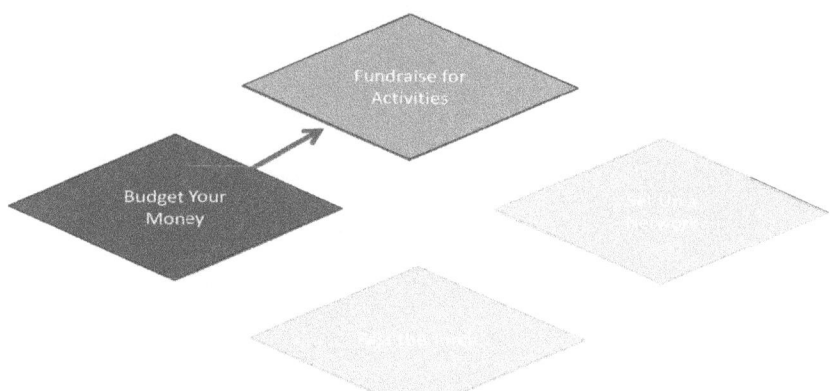

Fundraising is an essential element of bringing your program ideas to life. Most likely, the programs you would like to present require some type of financial support. Such things as advertisements, food, staging, AV equipment, etc. all require some sort of funds. An easy solution is to just have each member of your organization equally give his / her money to fund your programs. However, this is not likely because your organization will probably put on multiple programs throughout the academic year. Therefore, in this scenario, you will need a large financial commitment of money from your membership. This is a definite way to get members to leave your organization very quickly. Also, it is not an efficient use of your resources. Why would you pool your members for money when you have thousands of your fellow students, family, and friends that will give you money? This chapter will discuss many things to consider when establishing fundraisers for your organization. There is no golden solution presented in this chapter that will say, "The way to make X amount of dollars is doing Y." These are just things to consider when planning your next fundraisers and how to make them successful.

Why Do You Need Fundraisers?

At this point, your treasurer or finance person should have created a budget that describes the costs associated with all of the activities and programs for the academic year. As stated previously, you need funds to put on these events. **The primary goal of a fundraiser is to raise the money needed to fund your budget. The secondary goal is to make additional money that can be used towards the next academic school year.** After you recognize your need for fundraising, you must plan accordingly to successfully implement these fundraisers.

Planning

From your budget, you can set goals to know how much money you would like to raise from your fundraisers. For example, you are a member of the "Harry Potter Lovers United" organization and you would like to hold a "Harry Potter Ball." Your budget states that you need to raise $500 for all the decorations, food, music, etc... Therefore, your fundraising goal is to make a minimum $500 so that you can fund your "Harry Potter Ball."

From your goals, you have to decide how many fundraisers you would like to have over the course of the academic year. The total amount of money that you need to raise in the academic year will help you determine this. Also, the dates of the programs that you are having will be taken into consideration. Since you are raising money to put on programs, the fundraisers need to occur before the actual programs. Therefore, planning programs might need to be addressed again if the program date interferes with the fundraiser. If you have only one large program during one year, it should be towards the end of the academic year. Then you have the opportunity to break down your goals into multiple small size fundraisers. However, if you need the money sooner, you will need to have one large fundraiser. For example, to start off the academic year, you want to have the "Harry Potter Ball" the first weekend that school starts. As mentioned above, you need $500 to fund this event. In order to properly fundraise, you would need to have fundraisers before the first weekend of school. This can prove to be a very difficult task, because school has not begun. As stated, you need to have one large fundraiser to get the $500. On the other hand, let us say that you want to end the academic year with the "Harry Potter Ball", you have the entire academic year to raise the $500. You could possibly have five smaller fundraisers over the course of the academic year that raises $100 each in this way. This prevents you from trying to raise such a large amount at one time.

Fundraiser Sizes and Types

Fundraisers vary in sizes. Depending on your planning and goals, you may be able to do several small types of fundraisers or you could have a large fundraiser. **Small fundraisers are those that take a small effort to organize and yield a small profit.** An example of this would be a bake sale. Your members bake some delicious treats and sell them to the public for less than a $1 or just take donations. This requires little planning: you just need people to bake and show up to sell. However, you are probably not going to make much money. **Your large fundraisers are those that take a large effort to organize and yield a large profit.** An example of this would be putting on a concert. You need a lot of advertisements, booking a venue, security, etc…If it is successful, you could make a large profit. Depending on your organization's history and your campus's dynamics, it is difficult to say which are easier to do. If you are a new organization with a small membership (less than 10 people), it is simpler to do smaller size fundraisers. However, if your organization is larger and has been on campus for a long period of time, it may be more feasible to put on large types of fundraisers.

The majority of fundraisers typically work the same way. You are trying to get your peers, family, friends, etc. to donate money. It is important that they know the reason why they are giving you funds. This is why there are so many types of fundraisers that exist. They are all basically creative ways to get people to donate money.

One of the popular types of fundraisers is sales. Sales can be broken into products that your organization has made (such as baked items) or products that your organization has purchased from an external source (such as t-shirts). For products that your organization has made, make sure that items are safe and there is a need or want around campus for them. For example, if you are having a bake sale, only making bread with sugar on it is a bad idea. Despite the fact that you love sugar bread, there are many people that do not. This preference may cause weak sales.

Be sure to pay close attention to how you price your items/goods. You are trying to make a profit, so include costs when pricing items. By doing this, you set prices that make up the costs of putting on that fundraiser. This gives you the best opportunity for meeting fundraiser goals. Keep in mind that you do not want to overprice your goods. An example is trying to sell a brownie for $105 that was purchased for $5. Your goal for the fundraiser is to make a $100 profit. Therefore, you priced the brownie to meet your fundraiser goal. However, no one is realistically going to spend $105 for a brownie.

The other types of sales-based fundraisers are those that involve items bought from an external source. These are typically items that your organization buys in large quantities at a low price and sells to the public for a profit. An example of this is if you buy candy bars in bulk. You buy them at $1 per candy bar and sell them for $1.50 per candy bar. Another scenario is that you are selling items made by a company that takes a percentage of your profits. In both scenarios, keep in mind the prices you charge. It is easy to get greedy and want to charge large amounts of money to meet your profit goal. However, no one will buy overly expensive goods. Also, keep in mind the cost incurred by purchasing the goods that you are buying from the external source. For example, your fundraiser is selling t-shirts. Your profit goal is to make $500. You only bought 50 shirts. Therefore, you need to make a $10 profit on each shirt to meet your goal. You paid your supplier $20 to make the t-shirts. That means you have to charge $30 total per shirt to meet your profit goals. In many cases, people probably do not want to spend $30 on a t-shirt. So not only will you not make a profit, you will lose money since you already paid for the shirts. In this scenario, it would have been better to have bought cheaper shirts.

Additional Considerations

One of the factors that will help determine your specific fundraiser is the dynamics of your campus. In order to be successful, you must think about how your campus is structured and plan the best place to sell the items for the fundraiser's success. If you have a campus where students congregate in a central location, such as a student union, then you should plan fundraisers in that location since you have better chance at success. A larger volume of students in one location means that you have a greater opportunity to raise money. If your campus is a large commuter school, then you know that having fundraisers on the weekend may not be successful because there are not many on-campus residents. What time of day are most people on campus? If you have a large night-school population, then you might want to plan your fundraiser during the night time. Considerations such as these are helpful for determining the specifics of your fundraiser and what the best method of success will be.

Along with knowing how your campus works, you should understand the personalities of your members and their knowledge of the organization. As stated before, the primary goal of a fundraiser is to raise money needed to fund your budget, and possibly make additional money that can be used towards the next academic school year. Also, a fundraiser works as a way to get your peers, family, friends, etc. to contribute money. Since your members are the people who are helping to execute your fundraiser, they need to keep this in mind.

People give their money to fundraisers for two reasons: they want to buy the product or they want to support the organization. For people who want to buy a product, make sure your members have the necessary selling techniques and positive personalities that will appeal to these supporters. If you have some shy or introverted members, you may need to discuss selling techniques before you put them into a situation where they feel uncomfortable. Or you may want to give these individuals roles that are not associated with trying to get people to buy, such as designing or posting advertisements. In many situations, you only have a brief moment to attract someone's attention to get them to buy something. Therefore, you need dynamic members who are going to draw people.

For people who want to support your organization, make sure your members know enough information about your organization. If you are trying to sell something and a potential customer asks a question about your organization, it does not look good if your members have no idea how to answer. For example, an individual wants to give money to an organization that is selling jewelry, although they might think the jewelry is not attractive. Nevertheless, that person wants to support the organization. They ask about the event and where the proceeds will go. If the organization cannot answer that person, then he/she might be inclined to think that the organization is raising money for no direct reason. However, if they can articulate their reasons (i.e. they are raising money to fund a Harry Potter Ball), then the individual will have more of a reason to give money. That person may even give more than originally intended. If you are not sure of your member's knowledge of your organization or the goals of the fundraiser, then you may want to have a brief informational session about these topics during the meeting before your fundraiser.

Advertising

In order to get people to know your fundraiser is approaching, you need to make sure that you have effective advertising. With campus settings having so many fliers posted, you need to find a way to make your fundraising event stand out. Also, use as many advertising methods as possible to insure that you are going to reach as many people as possible so that your fundraiser is set up for success. Chapter 8 discusses advertising in more detail.

Paperwork

When planning your fundraiser, keep in mind that your campus may have paperwork that you need to complete beforehand. This usually is for renting equipment, permits to sell your items, etc. See your university's office that deals with student organizations. A list of more examples of fundraisers is shown in the appendix of the book

SET UP A NETWORK

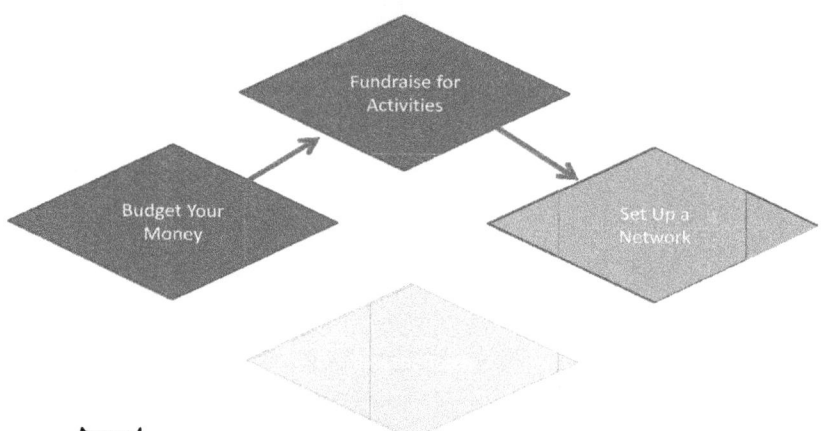

The phrase "Money, Power, and Respect" has been around for decades. This phrase can put an organization's success into a logical progression and help to sustain success. First you obtain the money, then you obtain the power, and finally you obtain the respect. This slogan can apply when forming a student organization. At Steps 9 and 10 your organization should have the *money* needed to do the things you want to do. The programs and events that you conduct from this money and the strong membership you built in Section 2 are what bring strength and *power* to your group: a powerful organization that now has influence on the campus community.

Now, it is time to gain the campus wide *respect* that you need in order to sustain your organization's greatness. True campus wide respect involves two areas: school staff and peers. This chapter will talk about the importance of respect in both realms and how to effectively obtain it.

Faculty and Staff Respect/Assistance

The downfall of many student organizations is that they never obtain the respect of the administration at their college or university. Some organizations think that as long as they have their peers' support they will be successful. These groups will probably have many successes; but in order to have sustainability, faculty and staff need to be a part of the network. The first person to contact when involving administration is your advisor. An advisor is a faculty or staff member that is knowledgeable about your cause and extremely interested in helping you fulfill your mission. An advisor's purpose is to support and to help make operations smoother on the administrative side. When faculty and staff hold meetings about campus organizations and student life issues, your advisor should be present to represent your group's interests. She/he is also there to make sure your organization is seen in a positive light among faculty and staff.

Not all organizations have an advisor; some universities do not even require you to have an advisor. However, it is extremely important to have a good, knowledgeable, and active advisor. If your university automatically appoints an advisor when you charter your organization with the school, make sure you talk to administration about why they chose him or her. You want to make sure that the person they assigned understands your mission and wants to be a part of it. If you are becoming a leader of an organization and you don't have an advisor, *get one!* Talk to your student organization office/personnel about the process of obtaining an advisor. Or if you have a person already in mind, feel free to schedule a meeting with him/her and ask this person to advise you. If you have an advisor who is inactive with your group, *find a new one!* The right advisor is crucial for an organization's success. It is alright to have an advisor that is not affiliated with the school as a supplement to your school advisor. However, you always need to have a faculty/staff advisor to benefit your organization.

Another important aspect of administration respect is getting to know your student organization office/personnel and other resources around campus. If you establish a good relationship with these people, your organization's life will be much easier. Student organization offices are usually the ones you have to approach for room scheduling, event approval, online event postings, flier ordering, etc. If you want your business done effectively, you need to stay in good standing with this office. Just think about it. If you are an organization of which they never heard, or if they have a negative perception about you, then you are going to be treated differently than a positive group who keeps in good contact with the office is treated. It is just human nature. Since this office is where you can get the most help for your organization in every aspect, it is important to maintain a good relationship which will allow you to get help and get your questions answered quickly. If you are in a bind and need support, you are much more likely to get it if the right people know and respect you.

Peer Respect and Networking

Gaining the respect and support from other students and other organizations is just as important as obtaining faculty and staff respect. In Step 8 the importance of ethics and staying in a positive light was discussed. This is the first step in ensuring that you have respect among your peers. Everyone needs to see you as being easy to work with and dedicated to your mission. The next step is networking and working with other organizations on campus. It is important to find other organizations that have similar interests and begin working with them in order to double your efforts. Recall in Step 1 when you were determining your need on campus. You researched the other organizations that already existed on campus to see if there were others like yours. In your findings you should have found organizations that are similar. These organizations are ones that with whom you should work. For example, if you are the Society for Hispanic Engineers and are going to put on a program to promote minorities in engineering, you should think about working with the Society for Black Engineers or the Society for Women Engineers on campus. This in turn doubles, or triples, your efforts making your events and cause more likely to succeed. Plus, this gains the respect of your fellow organizations and students which is necessary for the sustainability of your organization. In the future, those organizations will think of you when they are hosting a program or event.

Another way to gain respect and network with students is to have volunteers at events. It is not necessary to co-sponsor these events with others. The program may be too specific to your organization or other organizations may not have the time/resources to participate. In these cases or in large scale events like concerts, display ads and announcements that you need volunteers to help with the event. This does numerous things for your organization and the event itself. Doing this allows people who have no affiliation with your organization or other similar organizations to be a part of an event. Ask for people to be ushers, ticket takers, etc. This broadens your campus relationship and gives you a good reputation in the campus community, ultimately gaining you respect. This also could lead to more members joining the organization as well. More than likely if they are coming to help, they are interested in your mission which makes them a potential member. You should always co-sponsor programs if you can.

National Respect

As a last note it is important to talk about your affiliation with a national organization. This may not apply to all, but many campus organizations are affiliated with a country wide (sometimes worldwide) organization. This is almost always the case with Greek, athletic, and large scale academic organizations. Your campus organization, often referred to as a chapter, needs to work with its national affiliate. If there are national conferences or events, it is imperative that your organization be there in full support. Your organization will need the resources and respect of the national organization in order to ensure the longevity of the group. In many cases the national organizations filter down money, information, and support to the chapters only if they are in good standing. Similar to the points made earlier about faculty and staff, if you are a chapter of whom they are not acquainted, or have a negative perception, then you are going to be treated differently than a positive group who keeps in contact and stays in good standing. National affiliation goes beyond making contacts for career support. Although this is an excellent tool for making future business contacts, national networking is essential to your organization's success. It is necessary element for the sustainability of your organization.

So what about those organizations that do not have a national affiliation? It is recommended that you find something nationally that is similar to your group's mission. Even if the national organization does not directly line up with your mission, it may be close enough to become an affiliate. For example, take the Woman's Group against Oppression organization in Step 1. Surely they can find many groups around the country that have similar goals. They may not have the same name, but the mission and purpose will be very close. If you are having issues finding anything close to your organization, contact the student organization personnel or even nearby universities, and see if they have anything similar.

If not, you could consider starting one at other universities. Just follow the same steps you have been in this book at the other university. The outcome will be the same.

So in summary, respect is important in the sustainability of your organization. First, you get your budgeting and fundraising in order (money). Then, you recruit strong members and put on great events (power). Finally, you get the support of your faculty, staff, and peers (respect). Once you have all three elements, your organization will prosper.

PASS THE TORCH

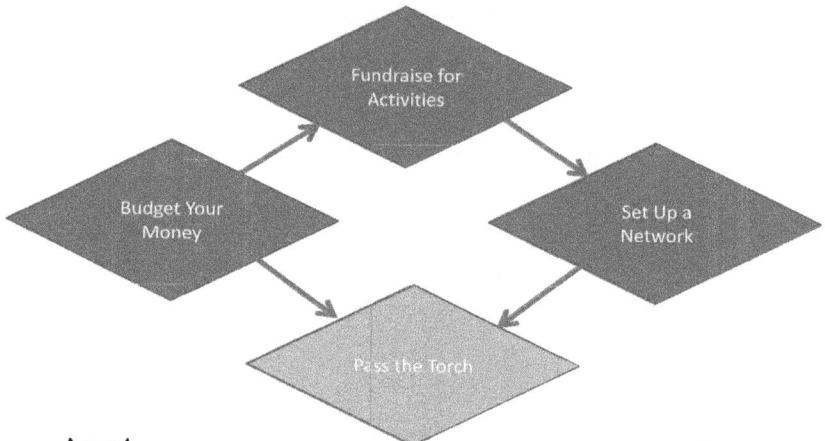

There comes a time in every organization when a leadership change will occur. This may be because of current officers graduating, transferring, etc. As mentioned in previous chapters, planning is one of the most important things that an organization can do. Recognizing that your leadership will not run the organization forever and planning to bring in new officers is an important aspect of running a successful organization. Remember that you should always be thinking about what is best for the organization. It can be very difficult to think about giving your leadership position to someone else, especially if you have had it for a couple of years. However, you must keep in mind the success you want your organization to have in the future and how much you want to see it grow. This is truly how a student leader leaves his /her legacy with an organization. This chapter will describe how to identify potential new officers and prepare them for leading your organization into the future.

Choosing New Officers

Choosing the right time to bring in new leadership differs with organizations. Every year, you should be holding some kind of event to choose new or re-elect current leadership. Normally, you want to hold elections towards the end of the academic year. You do not want to do this mid way through the year, as it will be too soon. However, you do not want to wait until the last week of school to do this either. You want to do it far enough in advance so that you can prepare the new officers for their positions, and be able to give enough advice about the current year's experiences.

When it is time to look at bringing in new officers, most likely the future leadership is going to be coming from your current members. This way, your future leadership will be able to use knowledge of the organization's past activities to make decisions regarding future planning. Also, it would be hard for your group to bring in officers from outside the organization and expect them to maintain the sense of community that has been developed at this point.

Everyone is not meant to lead. It is important to realize the difference between members who are potential leaders and members who are good workers. It is very easy to confuse the two. Making a mistake in this way could result in having new leaders that are not really prepared to be in leadership positions. This could hinder the growth of your organization. However, make sure you do not alienate members who you feel are not completely ready to be in leadership roles. As a leader, it is your responsibility to develop your members. Now we will discuss the different type of members you will encounter in your organization.

SECTION 3:
MAINTAIN YOUR ORGANIZATION

Type 1: The Soldier

During many activities of the organization you will notice several dedicated members who are very active. They show up to most of the meetings and are always available to help. Even though these individuals are very dedicated to your organization, they rarely speak up in meetings. They tend to be introverted and are not good at expressing their opinions. These are the members who would probably not be good as President and Vice-President. In leadership positions, you always want vocal people who will be able to express their opinions about the organization. So, it is up to your discretion to decide if they would fit. These are more of the kind of people who are great soldiers but potentially are not meant to lead just yet. Keep in mind that this is not a negative attribute. You will always need in your organization these "soldiers" who will participate in activities and volunteer. These types of people may have future leadership potential. You may encourage them to be more vocal in the organization and prepare them for being leaders in the future.

Type 2: The Talker

You may also notice members in your organization who are very vocal in meetings and activities, but do not participate to the level of the "soldiers." Talking without acting is not a quality you want in a leader. Leaders of an organization must develop great ideas and follow through on them. "The talker" has great potential for leadership because he/she knows how to voice ideas. However, he/she needs to learn how to take ownership of these ideas and act upon them by participating and being active in activities, which prepares them for leadership.

Type 3: The Attendee

These type of members show up to meetings but never say anything. Occasionally they may sign up for events, but you must constantly remind them to do things and meet deadlines. Extreme caution must be taken when thinking about these members for leadership positions. There is no reason to think that they are going to change just because they are elected to leadership positions. Either they need more time to develop in the organization, or they were not meant to lead.

Type 4: The Server

While there may be several members of your organization who are not ready to lead, there also may be some that are. These are the members who are dedicated to the organization and have expressed their opinions on many occasions. If asked, they also may give suggestions on things that they would like to see happen. Also, when needed, they are the people who help plan the event and do tasks efficiently. These are the people that are most likely to be future leaders of your organization. If you do not find these types of members in your organization, then you need to look for new members and spend extra time developing them into future leaders.

Forcing Members to Become Leaders

When deciding on the future leadership of your organization, it is important that the decision comes from the entire organization: both leadership and members. It is easy for the current leadership to just appoint new officers. However, this can cause problems within the organization. Some members can feel that they were passed over because of favoritism with the current leadership. Also, letting members decide their leadership lets them have a say in the direction of the organization.

SECTION 3:
MAINTAIN YOUR ORGANIZATION

If there are individuals that you feel will be good leaders, then you can suggest leadership opportunities to them through the year. Try not to overtly show favoritism and give them more privileges than other members. When there are leadership training programs or other opportunities, encourage these members to take advantage of those opportunities.

One of the best ways to choose new leadership (because it gives every member a fair shot at a position) is to have an election. The best way to have an election is to have individuals nominate candidates to positions and vote on each position. If you have a small organization, then you may only have one person running for a position. This makes it much easier to decide the new officers.

Preparation

After new officers are chosen, you must prepare them for their new roles. Usually, members only have a small idea of what each leadership position does. For example, they know that a Treasurer handles all financial decisions. However, they may not know that he/she also creates the budget for the year, handles travel arrangements to conferences, etc. Because of this, you will want the new leadership individuals to meet with the current person in that position. Then they can have a discussion describing the specifics of that position, describing past experiences in that position, and suggesting helpful hints for things they may not have known but wish they did. This makes sure that your new leaders are prepared for their positions and know what it takes to be successful. Also, suggest that the new leadership members have some sort of retreat or social outing so that they can become a closer unit.

As the academic year comes to a close, give the new leadership members an early experience in their new position. For example, if you elected a new president, let this person plan an agenda and facilitate an

Executive Board meeting. This will give the person a chance to discover possible areas of improvement before he/she actually takes office. Another example would be to have the newly elected secretary take meeting minutes and send out communications. This will give them experience of the tasks they will be doing in the upcoming academic year.

Staying Active After Leadership

After you have selected new officers, it is important to remember that you must still be present. It is important to stay active in the organization even after you are done servicing it as an officer. When you are still in the organization and after leaving office, be an active member and attend all meetings, events, etc. This shows the members that you have faith in the current leadership and you support their decisions. By not showing up to events without reason, it can be a sign that you are not comfortable with the organization's leadership. Also, do not become an open critic of the current leadership. Try to not discuss your opinions of the current leadership with members. Remember what it was like when you were in a new leadership position, and try not to criticize every decision they make. If you do have problems, try to address them to the new officers directly. Do not address them to the entire membership. Also, do not become too vocal in the meetings and activities. You still want to be active, but not dominating.

If you are graduating or leaving the university/college, you can still be an active alumnus of the organization. Be available to advise the current leadership about any planning that occurs. Your role now is to use your past experiences and knowledge to assist the new leadership. However, make sure that you are not forcing yourself on anyone. Give advice as needed and only when asked. You want to let them lead the organization into the future. Also, attend events and activities whenever possible. As an

SECTION 3:
MAINTAIN YOUR ORGANIZATION

alumnus, you can give current members excellent information regarding life after college. Also, do not forget to give back to your student organization monetarily. Alumni help organizations by donating money for programs and other activities. Be prepared to donate money and time to see the organization's continued success.

TROUBLESHOOTING – PROBLEM IDENTIFICATION

In any organization, business, family, or in life in general there will always be problems. It is impossible to completely remove all conflict from your organization. A leader must always be aware that at any moment in time, conflict can rear its ugly head. Since you cannot avoid it, learn how to deal with it. There have been numerous books written on problem solving and conflict resolution; so it is impossible for this one chapter to tell you how to deal with every issue that arises in your organization. Even if you have followed every step of this book and your organization is successful, you will still run into issues such as low membership morale, conflict with other organizations, internal group conflict, lack of program support, etc. It is recommended that you read other books about problem solving techniques. This chapter will attempt to give you the basic **problem identification** process that will work for nearly all of the situations you will encounter. The solution to the problem will be up to the leadership of the organization. Once you find the root cause, the solution will be easier to find then, and you will know you are truly fixing the problem.

The 5 Whys

Although it may seem "too simple", the 5 Whys technique has been used for decades by organizations, as well Fortune 100 companies. The 5 Whys is a simple problem solving technique made popular in the 1970s by the Toyota Production System. The strategy bases its solving capability around the questions: "Why?" and "What caused this problem?" Asking and answering the first "why", will bring about another "why." The answer from the second "why" will bring a third, and so on. Usually by the fifth why, you have found a suitable answer.

So let us apply this to a couple situations to make it seem clear.

Situation 1: The organization is losing members
1. **Why is the organization losing members?** Members are saying the meetings are pointless. When they do not come to meetings, they do not receive the information about the event dates and times.
2. **Why are they saying the meetings are pointless?** Since they only last 15 to 20 minutes, members would ask what is the point of coming?
3. **Why are meetings only 15 minutes long?** It is near the end of the year, and you have finished all programs.
4. **Why are you still meeting?** You are meeting because it is the regularly scheduled meeting time, and you think you still should meet.
5. **Why are you meeting just to meet?**

You started off with an issue of membership attendance: people were not coming to meetings and events. You may blame this behavior on the members, but you find out through the 5 Whys process that actually your meetings are the problem. Now, that you know the root cause, What do you do? It is up to you. The 5 Whys will not tell you how to fix the issue, but it will show you where to start. You could cancel the rest of the meetings for the year and just start up fresh the next year. Or a better idea is try to think of some innovative themes that can make your meetings more meaningful and fun to attend. Either way you are attacking the main issue.

TROUBLESHOOTING

Situation 2: The student organization office is unhappy with your organization

1. **Why is the student organization office unhappy with us?** You did not turn in your budget on time.
2. **Why didn't you turn in your budget on time?** The budget took more time to get together than you thought.
3. **Why did it take so much longer?** You underestimated the complexity of the job.
4. **Why did we underestimate the complexity of making a budget?** You made a quick estimate of the time needed to complete it, and the treasurer took on the responsibility himself without using other's help.
5. **Why did you make quick estimates and leave the issue up to one person to resolve?** You were running behind on other issues. You clearly need to review time estimation and task delegation procedures.

As you can see in this example, the organization missed the ball on turning in their budget on time. Most inexperienced organizations will just stop at the first why and just think that the group needs to be a little faster about turning in their information. As you go deeper however, you see that the true problem lies in the fact that your time scheduling/estimation procedures are flawed, and more importantly you are overloading your treasurer. You now know that with any large task you need to delegate work to others to assist your treasurer as depicted in the budgeting step (Step 9).

Finding the Optimal Solution

The 5 Whys strategy is an easy and often-effective tool for uncovering the root of a problem. Because it is so elementary in nature, it can be adapted quickly and applied to almost any problem. Bear in mind, however, that if it does not reveal an intuitive answer, other problem-solving techniques may need to be applied. Also, if you have not included your members in the process, your results may be useless. It is important to remember to include your members in both the problem identification and problem solution phases. Although you, as the leader, will have the final say as to what actions are taken, those actions need to be in line with your membership's best interests. If they are not, then you will be creating more of a headache for you and your organization. If they do coincide, you will be increasing the unity and strength of your organization.

There can be many solutions to any given problem. It is up to you (the leadership) and your members to find the optimal solution. **The optimal solution is the solution that solves the root cause of an issue and has the least amount of repercussion after implementation.** So, after you implement the solution, you should have very little negative effects on any other area of your organization. Deciding what the optimal solution is will take great time and effort, but it is critical to keeping an organization strong.

For example, look again at Situation 1 with declining membership. The root cause determined that the group was meeting just to meet. A couple of solutions that were introduced were to cancel the rest of the year's meetings or have meetings with more interesting and innovative topics. They both attack the root cause. Which idea is optimal? Let us look at the repercussions of each. If you cancel all the meetings, you may lose momentum for next year because you will lose touch with members early. Also, if you have any other programs for the year, how will you get your information out? On the plus side you may save money depending on if there are any costs associated with your meetings (food, prizes, activities etc.). The second idea of livening up the meetings also has its positives and negatives. A negative could be that the cost of meetings will go up because you are adding so much content to them to liven up the mood. Also, if the theme is too innovative, you may start to deviate from your mission. On the positive end you will definitely get more members to attend, which will increase moral. So which is optimal? That decision, as with every decision, will depend on money, membership interest, dedication/deviation from your mission, and many other factors. Prioritize what your organization deems important and choose the solution that affects the least amount and least important factors. Utilizing this critical thinking process is your best bet to finding the best solution and solving any issue that arises.

APPENDIX 1: FUNDRAISING LIST

As stated in Step 9, there is no universal solution to fundraisers. Organizations have varying levels of success with different fundraisers. The following list is an example of common possible fundraisers ideas that have been used by many organizations and found to be successful. There are many online resources. You can find detailed information as to how that particular fundraiser works.

Selling Cards
Pizza Cards
Restaurant Discount Cards
Scratch 'n' Give Cards

Selling Food
Baked Goods
Donuts
Candy Bars
Pizza Kits
Cookie Dough
Lollipops
Refrigerated/Frozen items

Offering Services
Tutoring
Babysitting
Holiday Gift Wrapping
Car wash

Selling Non-Food Items
Calendars
Candles
Christmas Wreaths
Holiday Baskets/ Flowers
Magazine Subscriptions
Christmas Ornaments

Organized Events
Recycled Can/Bottle Collection
Bowl – a – thon
Spare Change Collection
Silent Auction
Date Auction
Walkathon
Donations
Golf Outing
Parties

APPENDIX 2: BUDGET EXAMPLE

As stated in Step 9, a budget should be as complete as possible. There should be much discussion on detailing event specifics and break down costs. The following examples show budgets for an organization's plans for their winter semester activities. The first example shows a basic budget that lists the planned activity and the total cost. The second example shows a more itemized budget of the cost of the event.

Example 1

Winter Semester Activities	
Activity	Cost
Poetry Competition	$500.00
National Convention	$2,000.00
T-shirts for Membership	$200.00
Total	**$2,850.00**

APPENDIX 2

Example 2

Event	Budget Item	Total #	Cost per unit	Total Unit Cost
Poetry Competition	**Food**			
	Food Tray	1	$100.00	$100
	Prize			
	1st Place Gift Certificate	1	$100.00	$100
	2nd Place Gift Certificate	1	$50.00	$50
	3rd Place Gift Certificate	1	$25.00	$25
	Audio Visual Equipment			
	Microphone	1	$50.00	$50
	Stereo	1	$75.00	$75
	Advertisements			
	Flyers	100	$0.25	$25
	Campus Newspaper	1	$50.00	$50
	Web Ad	1	$50.00	$50
	Total			$500
National Convention	**Transportation**			
	12 passenger van ($50/day)	1	$350.00	$350
	Gas/Tolls	1	$300.00	$300
	Accommodations			
	Hotel 1 (110 for 4 nights)	4	$110.00	$440
	Hotel 2 (110 for 4 nights)	4	$110.00	$440
	Hotel 3 (110 for 4 nights)	4	$110.00	$440
	Van parking	1	$30.00	$30
	Total			$2,000
Meeting Advertisements	Buttons	100	$0.30	$30
	Media			$0
	Campus Newspaper	1	$25.00	$25
	Campus T.V.	1	$50.00	$50
	Web Ads	1	$20.00	$20
	Flyers	100	$0.25	$25
	Total			$150
T-Shirts for Membership	**T-Shirts**			
	S	20	$2.50	$50
	M	20	$2.50	$50
	L	20	$2.50	$50
	XL	20	$2.50	$50
	Total			$200
	GRAND TOTAL			**$2,850**

APPENDIX 3: AGENDA EXAMPLE

As stated in Step 6, an agenda is one of the most important aspects of a meeting because it outlines your thought process that will guide the meeting. There are many styles to writing an agenda, but all well-written agendas have six key elements:

Meeting Logistics

The date, time duration, and location of the meeting should begin the list when creating an agenda. This information helps members plan for attending a meeting when they are juggling school, homework, and social lives.

Expected Deliverables

At the end of most meetings there will be a list of tasks that certain people need to have done for the next meeting. At the beginning of the meeting you should review those deliverables. Make sure to clearly point out who is responsible and what needed to be done. This will add seriousness and responsibility to your meeting as well.

Old Business

Make sure to review any items not covered from the last meeting. Sometimes you cannot make it through everything on the agenda in one meeting, so cover them in the next meeting. Also, go over any events that occurred in between meetings and report their progress to the group.

New Business

This is the heart of your agenda. This is where you go over the progress on projects being performed by the group, current issues, preparation for events, etc. You should allot most of your meeting time to this part of the agenda.

Upcoming Events

Some organizations put this in the New Business section and others make it a separate part of the meeting. Either way, at some point in the meeting you need to remind the group about upcoming events: the time, location and date of the events.

Round Table and Other Campus events

At the end of every meeting you should allow the group to talk about whatever topics they want that affect the group. This is a time for anyone at the meeting to voice his/her opinion or ask for the group's support. Also, take some time to update the members on other events that are happening around campus, especially programs by other groups that you may want to work with in the future or have supported you in the past.

Lastly, some general notes about making a good agenda:
- List the time for every item on the agenda to keep it on track.
- Use clean formatting. Something like bullets or roman numerals works well.
- Try not to get to wordy. Keep every item simple but broad enough to convey the message.
- Make sure to send out the agenda with the meeting notice. This gives the group a chance to review and prepare for the meeting topics.
- Keep your agenda style consistent from meeting to meeting. This shows meeting seriousness and gets your group accustomed to your meeting style.

An example of a good agenda for the *Computer Gamers Club* is shown on the next page.

APPENDIX 3

Examples

The Computer Gamers Club

Agenda for 08/08/2008
Time: 6pm – 8pm,
Location: Coleman Computer Lab – 2EW40

> Clearly list the time, location and date of the meeting.

I. **Expected Deliverables** – 6pm

> Clearly list who is responsible for what.

  a. **John** – Copies of the new *Battle Oger* game for Monday's *Game Night* event
  b. **Amy** - Fliers for Monday's *Game Night* Event
  c. **ALL** – Ideas for Fundraisers

II. **Upcoming Events** – 6:15pm

  a. *Game Night* – 08/11/2008
  b. *Campus Student Organization Meeting* – **08/27/2008**
  c. *Budgets due for 2009 School year* – **11/08/2008**
  d. *National Gamers Conference* - Phoenix, Arizona - **12/12/2008**

III. **Old Business** – 6:45pm

> Always review the last meeting. The most efficient meeting is to just briefly go over the minutes.

  a. *Approval of last meeting's minutes*
  b. **Recognition for an Excellent job on last week's event!**

> Show the time for each item. This will keep your meeting on task and on time.

IV. **New Business** – 7:00pm

  a. Committee updates:

> Provide sufficient time to allow your members and committees to give updates.

   i. **Public Relations Committee** – Progress on new Campus TV promotion
   ii. **Membership Committee** – Recruitment plans for next semester
   iii. **Game Supply Committee** – New Agreement with Blockbuster®
  b. *Next meeting – 08/15/2008 @ 6pm*
   i. Review of the presentation for the Campus Student Organization meeting on 08/27/2008 – Presented by John Doe
   ii. **ALL PAYMENTS FOR THE NATIONAL CONFERENCE ARE DUE!!!**

V. **Misc** – 7:50pm

  a. Brian's Birthday party this weekend
  b. The Video Game Club is having a game night tonight at 9pm

> Remember to talk about things that are happening on campus and ask your members to show support at other events.

VI. **Round Table** – 7:55pm

> Allow time for a round table to let the members speak their minds.

ADJOURN!!!

94

APPENDIX 4: PROGRAM CHECKLIST EXAMPLE

Below is a general program checklist. This is just a guideline for you and your organization to use in order to have a successful program. The authors of this book do recommend that you use a checklist when putting on a program. A checklist allows you to be organized and keeps you on task to ensure a great program. In addition, the checklist helps to keep you and your organization on track as you move forward with all the intricacies of a program.

Let us take a look below at the items on the checklist. First, be sure to reserve your venue/ room early. Remember you are not the only campus organization putting on programs, and you do not want to have an unsuccessful event because of improper preparation. Second, determine the rules and standards that you will have for the program. For example, are you having a special speaker for a program? Do you want the public to ask questions to the speaker or do you want people to just listen? Next, be sure to get a commitment from volunteers and members to work the event. Verify that they are ok with the shift schedule that you will develop. Arranging volunteers will be a task depending on the schedule of volunteers and students. The day before the event send out a quick reminder email. As a student leader you should have an idea of the number of participants and attendees that will be at the program. This will help determine if extra chairs, tables, etc. are needed to accommodate spectators. Do not forget to reserve equipment and check equipment at the event to make sure it WORKS!

During your activity, promote it to other students and supervise operations. This is your program and you want to make sure it is successful. At the end of your activity make sure that your program accomplished its goal by getting feedback from attendees. Hand out surveys to attendees or develop an electronic survey and send it out via

APPENDIX 4

email. Sit down with the Core 4 and perform a cost benefit analysis. At this time you should be asking if your labor and planning help develop and execute an effective program. And finally **HAVE FUN!!** If you are not having fun, it will not be a great program.

APPENDIX 4

Examples

	Program Checklist	TimeFrame
1	Reserve a room or venue(i.e. Gymnasium) where the program will be held.	4 wks before the event
2	Determine the rules/standards for the program.	2 weeks before event
3	Get a commitment from members/volunteers that will be able to work shifts during the program.	2 wks before the event
4	Create a shift schedule for members/volunteers and verify schedule.	2 weeks before event
5	Create advertisements (flyers, word of mouth, Internet, TV , Radio,).	2 wks before the event
6	Determine how many participants or attendees will be at the activity.	1 wk before the event
7	Reserve equipment for the program (AV Equipment, Microphones, Chairs, TV etc.).	3 days
8	Send a reminder email or message to students about the event.	1 day before the event
9	Setup room.	2 hours before event
10	Check equipment and make sure you have the items you reserved.	2 hours before event
11	Promote event to students during the event.	During Event
12	Supervise operations of event.	During Event
13	Determine final profit projections by performing cost benefit analysis.	After event
14	Evaluate the event based on profits, membership feedback, and participant feedback.	After event
15	Have Fun.	All the Time

97

APPENDIX 5: FLIER EXAMPLE

The next few pages will cover two flier examples. The first example, located on the next page, is how not to use a flier. Notice that the title of the event is not engaging. In addition, the logistics of the event are not clearly stated. For example, where is the event? What time is it? Do participants win anything? These are some things that student organizations forget to add to a flier. Be sure to pay attention to the artwork: It is too big and takes away from the name and symbol of the organization. Finally, make sure to use spell check and find a person to review your flier, before posting them.

APPENDIX 5

Name of event is not creative. Artwork is too big.

gistics
event
e not
lear.

Video Game Tourney

When: May 21ˢᵗ, 2008

Who: Any and All Football Video Game Players

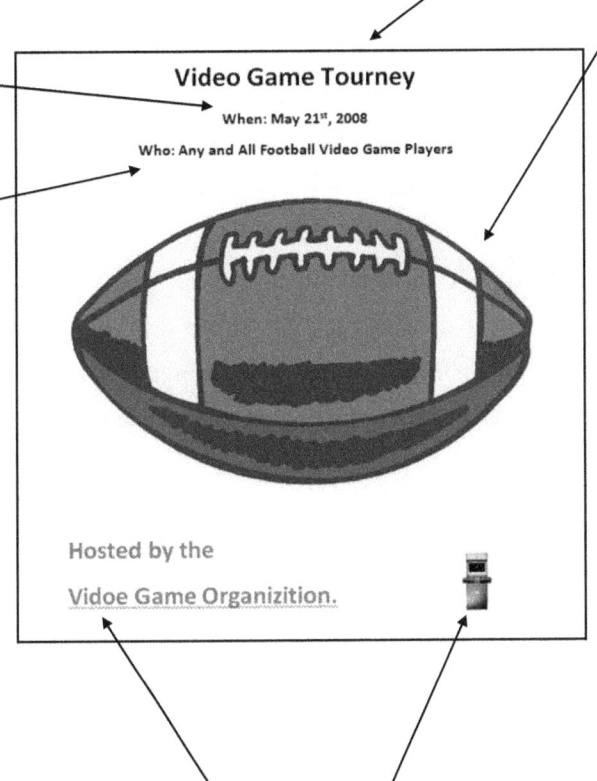

Hosted by the

Vidoe Game Organizition.

Name of organization is spelled wrong. Symbol of Organization is not prominently displayed.

APPENDIX 5

The next flier is a great example. Notice that the flier contains all the information that was stated in Step 8. The name of the organization is prominently displayed in the middle of the flier. You can increase the size of the name if you wish, however be careful because you do not want to distract from your event. The logistics of the event are also covered in the example. The time, location, and date of the event are clearly posted. In addition, participants know that there is a prize at the end of the tournament. Finally, the flier is creative and unique. If you wish to differentiate yourself, print fliers on different colored paper to really make your advertisement unique. How about actually advertising your event with a t-shirt? Have the event imprinted on t-shirts purchased by your organization. Your members will become living billboards, and people will notice them.

APPENDIX 5

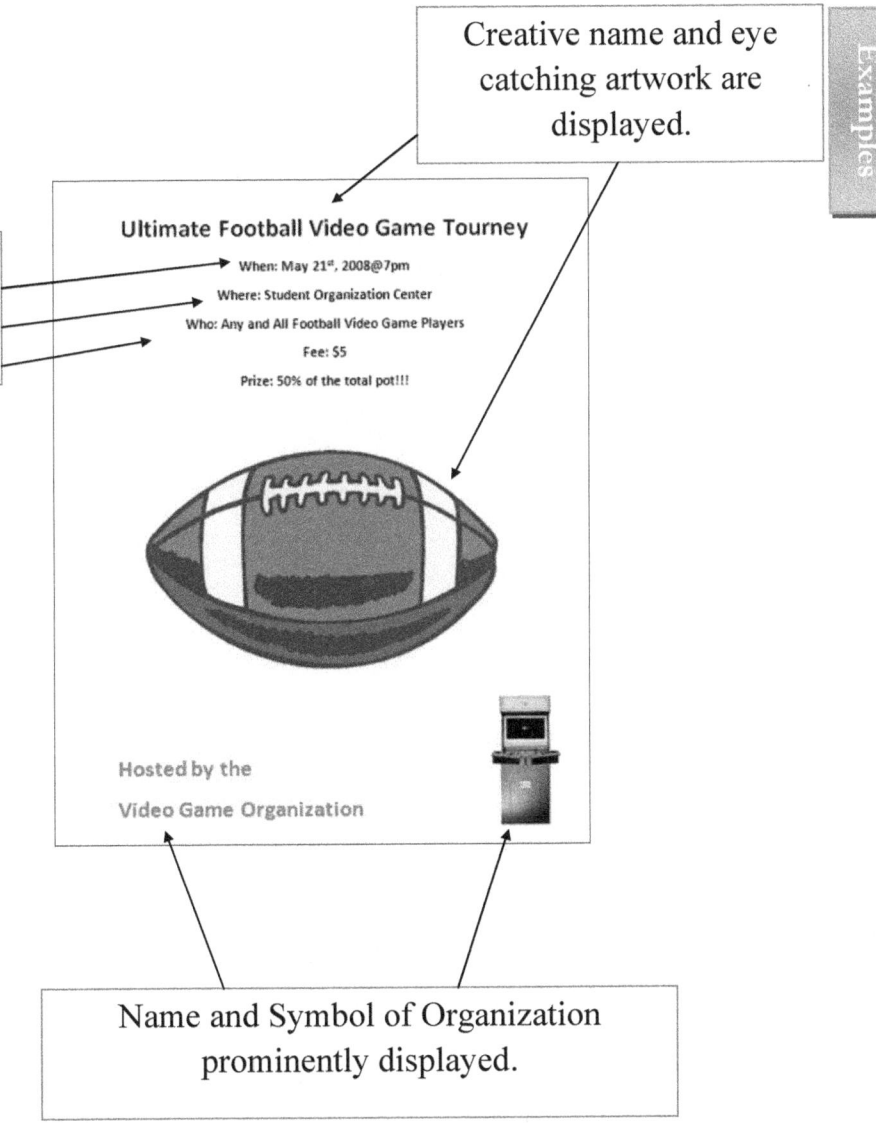

www.ingramcontent.com/pod-product-compliance
Lightning Source LLC
Chambersburg PA
CBHW032130090426
42743CB00007B/539